DEATH
IN EARLY
NEW ENGLAND

DEATH IN EARLY NEW ENGLAND

RITES, RITUALS AND REMEMBRANCE

ROBERT A. GEAKE

THE
History
PRESS

Published by The History Press
Charleston, SC
www.historypress.com

Front cover, top: Winsome angel carved by Henry Emmes on the gravestone of Elizabeth Greene, family cemetery, Spring Green Farm, Warwick, Rhode Island. *Photo by author. Bottom*: Overview of Plymouth 1622, from Powell's *Historic Towns of New England* (1896).
Back cover: Gravestones of Lydia and Stephen Parker, Plain Meeting House Cemetery, West Greenwich, Rhode Island. *Photo by author.*

First published 2023

Manufactured in the United States

ISBN 9781467154789

Library of Congress Control Number: 2023932155

Notice: The information in this book is true and complete to the best of our knowledge. It is offered without guarantee on the part of the author or The History Press. The author and The History Press disclaim all liability in connection with the use of this book.

This book is dedicated to the memory of my grandmother
Jennie Fernald Kenney (1889–1979),
who dedicated her adult life to nursing and her patients

CONTENTS

PREFACE

Death was prevalent in early New England from the moment the first Europeans began settlements along the shore of what would become Plymouth Colony. Those first settlers in 1620, after months of meandering, would not decide on a location until December, when food and ale on the ship *Mayflower* had grown scarce. The Pilgrims, as they were called from the earliest writings, did not begin building "the first house for common use" until the twenty-fifth of the month. Cotton Mather's description would be widely distributed in his *Magnalia Christi Americana:*

> *The* Hardships *which they encountered, were attended with, and productive of* deadly sickness; *which in two or three Months carried off more than* Half *their Company. They were but meanly provided for against these unhappy* Sicknesses; *but there died sometimes* Two, *sometimes* Three *in a Day, till scarce* Fifty *of them were left alive; and of those* Fifty, *sometimes there were scarce* Five *well at a time to look after the sick.*

In April, when the remaining settlers could look forward to planting, their governor died from the effects of apparent heatstroke after working in the fields on an unusually hot spring day. William Bradford would write, "He was buried in the best manner they could, with some volleys of shot by all that bore arms. And his wife, being a weak woman, died within five or six weeks of him."[1]

View of Burial Hill, Plymouth, Massachusetts. *Photo by author.*

Bradford himself had come close to death and was still sick when elected governor to replace the fatally stricken John Carver.

Those first settlers who died were buried on the hill above the street where the first houses would be constructed. It would later become known as Cole's Hill, for tavern keeper John Cole, who owned the location in the 1640s. Plymouth's Burial Hill would be established as the town cemetery in 1637.

Later generations would fare little better through waves of seasonal illness and epidemics that were common well into the eighteenth century. Disease, in some cases, erased entire families and almost always affected the majority of individuals in the communities it touched.

Death occurred also from a variety of accidental causes as well as from infirmities, old age and childbirth, without discrimination between those poor or wealthy of the community.

Most commonly, young mothers mourned the loss of infants, but in the worst situation, they might also die with the child, as did twenty-year-old Sarah Updike in 1718, wife of Daniel Updike, the young scion of the Updike family, whose early homestead was a large plantation above Wickford, Rhode

Island. The tragic loss of mother and infant would be written on her grave by the grieving family:

> *Within this tomb lyeth buried Sarah the youngest daughter of Benedict Arnold of this island gentleman and of Sarah his wife. She was married to Daniel Updike of Narraganset and deceased in travail of their first child who lyes also here intered. This delectable body received its birth November the 3rd 1698 and submitted to inexorable death January the 26th 1717/8. Here lyes the casquet but the jewels gone, guided by angels to the almighty throne to live forever with the Three in One.*[2]

Parents could gain hope for their child's survival if they lived through their first few waves of fevers and fugues that accompanied each winter and spring in New England.

Death was so prevalent in early New England that it marked the generations who continued and grew the settlements into villages and towns. Little wonder that such sadness pervaded a life of work, worship and remembrance, that such emotion is wrought in the carvings and effigies carved on the stones to keep their memory.

This book will explore death in early New England: its causes, those rituals that came and evolved to remember the dead and the memorials and epitaphs that can still be found on the grounds of New England cemeteries.

I began this work when our nation, and indeed the entire world, was in the throes of the worst pandemic in a century. My hope is that readers who have suffered loss over the past three years, as my own family has, will take comfort in the resilience shown by earlier generations and their conviction that science and faith would conquer whatever pestilence came to their communities and that the ancient adage "this too shall pass" would prove once again that wisdom and provide the certainty that they would endure.

A WORD ABOUT LANGUAGE: I have quoted texts verbatim from their seventeenth- and eighteenth-century sources throughout this book so that the reader may appreciate the language of the day and the context in which it was written.

CHAPTER 1

THE LAW IN EARLY NEW ENGLAND, CAPITAL CRIMES AND PUNISHMENT BY DEATH

Crime in early New England was largely believed to be a manifestation of "the Devil's work," most often inspired by drunkenness, lasciviousness, avoiding church on the Sabbath and even possession by witchcraft. The laws drafted in the early colonies were adaptations of English laws that these settlers had lived under before, and thus they had familiarity with the punishments meted out. Petty crimes, such as pickpocketing, fornication, slander and trespass, were often punished with fines or being placed in the stocks. Serious offenders might be tied to a post for whipping, tied to a chair fixed on a long pole for dunking in a stream or pond or endure various other methods of public humiliation. Those who committed capital crimes such as murder, infanticide, witchcraft, sodomy, rape and even burglary could expect more serious forms of punishment, including the sentence of death.

Plymouth Plantation, during its fledgling years of 1620–30, was hardly the harmonious settlement portrayed in early histories printed in the new republic. Religious and civil discord began to plague the colony soon after those who had survived the first winter began to plant and prepare a civil contract to establish law among the soon-to-be-burgeoning population, which included religious seekers, investors and others arriving with patents from England. These patents and claims to land were often dubious at best and brought with them trouble in the form of strong-minded individuals who had obtained them by some means and had little regard for the colony's attempts to establish civil order.

Overview of Plymouth, 1622. *Powell's* Historic Towns of New England *(1896)*.

One such individual was Thomas Morton, an associate and one-time scribe for Isaac Allerton, an investor who arrived with a patent providing him with lands that stretched into the area known today as Quincy, Massachusetts. Morton convinced a number of newly arrived individuals to establish their own plantation in the territory where they could live as they chose, without the cumbersome civic responsibilities that Plymouth had imposed on its citizens. Bradford recounts the inevitable result:

> *After this, they fell to great licentiousness and led a dissolute life, pouring out themselves into all profaneness. And Morton became Lord of Misrule, and maintained (as it were) a school of atheism. After they had got some goods into their hands, and got much by trading with the Indians, they spent it as vainly in quaffing and drinking, both wine and strong waters in great excess....They also set up a Maypole, dancing and drinking about it many days together, inviting the Indian women for their consorts, dancing and frisking together like so many fairies, or furies rather, and worst practices.*[3]

Morton also illegally traded shot, powder and firearms with the Indigenous people, trained them in the amount of shot needed to kill fowl or deer and then employed them as hunters to bring game to his own table. With so much leisure time, he became a prolific composer of lewd verses and lyrics, some, as Bradford wrote, "tending to lasciviousness," while others skewered the moral character of individuals in Plymouth.

Morton authored a three-volume critique of the colony in 1637 entitled *New England Canaan*, which, like Roger Williams's *Key into the Language of America*, often portrayed the Indigenous people and their culture in a more flattering light than other prominent European settlers. Morton especially decried Plymouth's attempt to create what he called a New Israel, meaning one confined to the strictness of Old Testament, or Jewish law as transcribed in the Bible.

Authorities in both Plymouth and Boston soon became alarmed with Morton's behavior and influence on other would-be settlers and investors. When he became the prime suspect in the murder of one of these investors, a warrant was issued for his arrest. Captain Miles Standish, who had previously dealt so brutally with Indigenous leaders wary of signing any treaty with the colony, was sent with a posse of men to take Morton by force and bring him back to Plymouth. Bradford wrote that when they arrived at his house,

> *they found him standing stiffly in his defense, having made fast his doors, armed his consorts, set divers dishes of powder and bullets on the table; and if they had not been over-armed with drink, more hurt might have been done.*

Morton and his followers held a standoff at the house, scoffing at those who had come to arrest them. Fearing an assault on the house, the men came out with the intention of engaging Standish and his deputies in a gunfight, but as Bradford recorded,

> *they were so steeled with drink as their pieces were too heavy for them.... Neither was any hurt done to any of either side, save that one was so drunk that he ran his own nose upon the point of a sword that he held before him.*[4]

Morton and others were brought back, placed in irons and imprisoned on a ship offshore until it took Morton back to England. He would later return and settle in the wilderness of what would become Maine.

That same year, William Bradford recorded the occasion of the colony's first execution for murder, in September 1630:

> *This year John Billington the elder, one that came over with the first, was arraigned, and both by Grand and Petty jury found guilty of willful murder, by plan and notorious evidence. And was for the same accordingly*

Plymouth courthouse, built on the site of Edward Winslow's house where Billings gave testimony. *Photo by author.*

> *executed. This, as it was the first execution amongst them, so it was a matter of great sadness....They used all due means about his trial and took the advice of Mr. Winthrop and others* [of] *the ablest gentlemen in the Bay of Massachusetts, that were then newly come over, who concurred with them that he ought to die, and the land be purged from blood.*
>
> *He and some of his had been often punished for miscarriages before, being one of the profanest families amongst them; they were from London, and I know not by what friends shuffled into their company. His fact was that he waylaid a young man, one John Newcomen, about a former quarrel, and shot him with a gun, whereof he died.*

Billington had been among the others to arrive on the *Mayflower*, and he had many friends among the small community. The confrontation with the victim came about because Billington rightly suspected that Newcomen was stealing from his traps. His reputation as a good hunter also belied the facts about the shooting, as the victim was shot haphazardly in the shoulder while fleeing the scene; though the accused reputedly would let no other take responsibility. His written confession sealed his fate, and he was the first man to be hanged in the colonies.

Law and order in Massachusetts Bay Colony consisted of a "general court," or assembly of stockholders in the colony that yearly elected a governor and assistants at the meetinghouse in Boston until 1634, when it was decided that

> *four General Courts should be kept every year, and that the whole body of freemen should be present only at the Court of election as magistrate, and that, at the other three, every town should send their deputies, who should assist in making laws, disposing lands, etc.*[5]

Two years later, the structure of the court was amended once again:

> *It was ordered that a certain number of the magistrates should be chosen for life....It was likewise ordered, that quarter courts* [courts that met on a quarterly basis] *should be kept in several places for ease of the people, and, in regard of the scarcity of victuals, the remote towns should send their vote by proxy to the court of elections.*

In that same year, 1636, Winthrop convened with minister John Cotton, "being requested by the General Court, with some other ministers in compiling a body of fundamental laws." These were based on both Old Testament biblical law and the common English laws imported from Great Britain's judiciary.

AN ENTRY IN HIS Winthrop's journal from June 1641 shows that the colony was still struggling to interpret biblical tenets to sanction civic law:

> *There arose a question in the Court about the punishment of single fornication, because, by the Law of God, the man was only to marry the maid, or pay a sum of money to her Father; but the case falling out between two servants, they were whipped for the wrong offered to the master in abusing his house; and were not able to make him other satisfaction.*
>
> *The like difficulty arose about a rape, which was not death by the Law of God, but because it was committed by a boy upon a child of 7 or 8 years old, he was severely whipped. Yet it may seem by the equity of the law against sodomy, that it should be death for a man to have carnal copulation with a girl so young...For it is against nature as well as sodomy and buggery.*[6]

In 1642, Plymouth faced its first case of bestiality when seventeen-year-old Thomas Granger confessed to committing the crime numerous times with at least a dozen animals. He was sentenced to watch the beasts he had fornicated with be slaughtered, and then he himself was executed.[7] Such punishment was an example of extracting the law from the Old Testament of the Bible, which states in the book of Leviticus that if "any man or woman shall lie with any beast or brute creature" they should be put to death and that "the beast shall be slain and buried and not eaten."[8]

Such cases were, of course, exceedingly rare, but among the more prevalent crimes in the colonies were trespass, burglary and theft. While in rural areas, farms and businesses were widely spread, the growing population in established towns, where poverty became at times particularly brutal, contributed to an increase in crime.

The early criminal code of the Massachusetts Bay Colony instructed that those convicted of burglary "be strictly punished," but the sentence was left to the discretion of the judge before whom the case was tried. By 1647, however, the sharp increase in these crimes caused the authorities to revise the punishments: first-time offenders were branded with a *B* on the forehead, a second conviction brought the punishment of a second branding as well as being "severely whipped" and a third conviction brought the sentence of death.

The code of law became known as the "Body of Liberties" and was distributed to each town in the colony.

When the Massachusetts Bay Colony merged with Plymouth County in 1692, the newly named Province of Massachusetts Bay adopted the laws of the original Bay Colony, with amendments that stipulated those convicted a second time for burglary receive thirty-nine lashes. While the law still recommended the death penalty for a third conviction, it gave the court the authority to sentence those convicted to be "otherwise grievously punished."[9]

These prescribed punishments for burglary and theft were not amended to lesser sentences until 1839, when these offenses were no longer considered capital crimes.

Neighboring colonies varied in the punishment meted out for such crimes and seem also to have had prescribed measures, or tiers, of punishment according to the severity of the theft. On September 24, 1713, Joshua Hempstead of New London, Connecticut, recorded in his diary: "I was in Town in ye forenoon to See a man Branded on ye forehead for breaking open a house in Lebanon & Stealing Sundrys &c."[10]

The early court system of Providence was established in its first code of law in 1640, with a body of "ffive desposers" to "meete upon gennerall ocations" and look after those instances where "any person abuse another in person or goods."

The colony had been founded in 1636 by Roger Williams, a religious and civic philosopher who believed in "soul liberty," or the right to one's own spiritual beliefs without threat of punishment from the governing body.

Williams believed in a governing body made up of the citizens who lived in the colony. Such self-rule was viewed by the king of England as a "lively experiment" in the colonies when he granted a royal charter. Though Roger Williams believed in spiritual freedom, he also believed in a strict code of law as well as what some today would consider excessive punishment for the variety of crimes it encompassed.

At the "Generall Court," in 1640, the first governing body in the colony decreed that "each Towne shall provide a Towne Book, wherin they shall Record the Evidence of the Lands by them impropriated; and shall also have Powre to give forth a Coppie thereof." And in the same decree,

> It is ordered, that a Booke shall be provided, wherein the Secretery shall write all such Lawes and Acts, as are made and constituted by the Body, to be left always in that Towne…and also that copies of such Acts as shall be made now, or hereafter, at the Generall Courts concerning necessary uses and ordinances to be observed, shall be fixed upon some public place where all men may see and take notice of them.[11]

By the year 1648, another decree was recorded in the town's *Book of Brass Clasps*, the first such book of records, entitled "The Progress in Law," its first tenet being,

> All actions and cases shall be tried by six townsmen in the nature of a jury, yet with the liberty of not being put on swearing; and these six men to be picked by the town quarterly, and warned three days before the court, by the Sergeant, to be ready at the day and hour appointed, under penalty of three shillings for their neglect.[12]

As might be expected, the code of law adapted listed individual rights as the government's most important mandate. Rhode Island was first of the colonies to declare that "the forme of Government in *Providence Plantations* is DEMOCRATICAL"; the first order in the civil code reads:

Providence's *Book of Brass Clasps*. *Courtesy of the Rhode Island State Archives*.

That no person, in this Colonie, shall be taken or imprisoned, or be disseized of his Lands or Liberties, or be Exiled, or any other otherwise molested or destroyed, but by the Lawful judgement of his Peeres, or by some known Law. [13]

As for common law, the code consisted of five general laws, declaring that of the offenses, "murdering Fathers and Mothers being ye highest and most unnatural," but also included "High Treason, Pettie Treason, Rebellion, Misbehavior and their accessories." Among other crimes that faced severe punishment were witchcraft, burning of houses, forcible entry, rape, adultery and fornication. [14]

Rhode Island also dealt burglars harsh sentences. The first to be given the death sentence for that crime in the colony was William Thomas in May 1671. After robbing a silversmith's shop in Boston, he was caught with "one silver wine cup unmarkt, one silver Bodkin Marked M.B., two silver sawes [knives] spoones with forks at the other ends" and a silver plate. He pled not guilty but, under examination, owned that he had robbed the smith and so was sentenced to be hanged.

After reviewing his "earnist peticion," the court delayed his sentence until he was hanged on June 9, 1671. This was a common humane gesture by judges and governors of the time, allowing the condemned man or woman time to reflect on their crimes and prepare themselves spiritually for their end on earth.

The case, however, proved to be more complicated. In October 1671, the court indicted Elinor Boomer, wife of Matthew Boomer, on three charges, one of which accused her of enabling an Indigenous man named Robin, who had been convicted of larceny, to escape prison. A second charge was that she acted to "perswade and abet" William Thomas to "Rob and Steale," the third that she "did Receive keepe and conceal several goods stolen by William Thomas from Mr. Kemble a smith in Boston."

While she was found not guilty of the first two charges, she was found "guilty of concealing goods," according to the Bill of Indictment. [15]

The colony of Connecticut established eleven initial laws called the Fundamental Orders in January 1639, establishing a formal confederation among the settlements within its territory, as the preamble to the document states:

For as much as it hath pleased Almighty God by the wise disposition of his divine providence so to order and dispose of things that we the inhabitants of

Windsor, Hartford, and Wethersfield are now cohabitating and dwelling in and upon the River of Connectecotte and the lands thereunto adjoining; and well knowing…the word of God requires that to maintain the peace and union of such a people there should be an orderly and decent Government established according to God, to order and dispose of the affairs of the people at all seasons as occasion shall require.[16]

As with Massachusetts law, there was no separation between the church and civil law as had been established in neighboring Rhode Island, whose loose compact of law between settlements was looked on warily by New England authorities. These Fundamental Orders would be the rule of law in Connecticut until 1650, when legal scholar Roger Ludlow created the Code of 1650, borrowing language from both the Massachusetts Bay "Body of Liberties" as well as the Magna Carta:

Forasmuch as the free fruition of such Libberties, Immunities, Privelages, as Humanity, Civillity and Christianity call for, as due to every man in his place and proportion without Impeachment and infringement, hath ever beene and ever will bee the Tranquilty and Stability of churches and Common wealths, and the denyall or deprival thereof, the disturbance if not ruine of both:

It is therefore ordered by this Courte and Authority thereof, that no mans life shall bee taken away, no mans honor or good name shall bee stained, no mans person shall be arrested, restrained, banished, dismembered nor in any way punished; no man shall be deprived of his wife and children, no mans goods or estate shall bee taken away from him, nor in any ways indamaged, under colour of Law or countenance of Authority, unless it bee by the virtue or equity of some express Law of the Country warranting the same.[17]

And express laws there were in explicit detail throughout the code, the longest and most restrictive having to do with the Indigenous peoples that remained around the settlements.

Brief descriptions of each are as follows:

It is ordered and decreed by this Court and Authority thereof, that…every person shall duley resorte and attend thereunto respectively upon the Lord's day, and upon such publique fast days and days of Thanksgiving as are to bee generally kept by the appointment of Authority. And if any person within this jurisdiction shall without just and necessary cause withdraw himself from hearing the publique ministry of the word, after due meanes of conviction used, he shall forfeit for his absence from every publique meeting, five shillings: All such offences to be heard and determined by any one Magistrate or more, from time to time.[18]

Perhaps with the well-known actions of Thomas Morton and his followers in the early Bay Colony in mind, the code addressed the dangers of idleness among the settlements:

No person, howseholder or other, shall spend his time idlely or unprofitably, under paine of such punishment as the Courte shall thinke meet to inflict: and for this end, it is ordered, that the Constable of every place shall use special care and diligence to take knowledge of offenders of this kinde, especially of common Coasters (drifters), unprofitable fowlers (casual hunters), and Tobacko takers, and present the same unto any Magistrate, who shall have power to heare and determine the case or transfer it to the [next] Courte.

Innkeepers were also required to follow strict laws and regulations because of those "many abuses of that lawful liberty." Under penalty of five shillings for every drunken individual, they were required to limit drinking to excess, serving "about half a pointe [pint] of wyne for one person at a tyme, or to continue tippling aboute the space of halfe an houre, or at unseasonable times, or after nine of the clock at night." The innkeeper faced placement in the stocks or imprisonment if these rules were not followed, though the law did permit him or her to serve and entertain "seafaring men or land travelers in the night season [winter] when they come first on shoare, or from theire voyage or journeye, for theire necessary refreshment."[19]

Witchcraft

The code also sought to remedy the fear that was foremost in colonial settlers' minds, that of witchcraft, or of those healers and outcasts who might sign a pact with the devil and cause illness in a family or cast a spell of death on the livestock they owned. Such witches could change shape and form and were most commonly seen as black cats, dark birds in the forest or even wolves.

The belief in witchcraft and the subsequent suspicions that fell on elderly women in particular were another unfortunate tradition brought from Great Britain to her colonies in North America. However, as historian David Hackett Fisher has pointed out, "Adult women accused of witchcraft tended to be younger" in the colonies. "In England a witch was most often in her 60s; in America, she was in her 50s."[20]

The first notation of a conviction of witchcraft in Massachusetts comes from Winthrop's *Journal* and an entry in May 1648, which reads, in part,

> *At this Court one Margaret Jones of Charlestown was indicted and found guilty of witchcraft, and hanged for it. The evidence against her was this. I. That she was found to have such a malignant touch, as many persons (men, women, and children) whom she stroked or touched with any affection or displeasure, or, etc., were taken with deafness, or vomiting, or other violent pains or sickness.*[21]

In addition to this evidence, Jones procured her own herbs and concocted medicines that had "extraordinary violent effects." She warned those who refused to purchase her medicines that they would not be healed, and indeed, their sickness worsened. Along with this evidence presented was the fact that "some things which she had foretold came to pass accordingly."

Such witches, as the unfortunate accused, were common by the second or third generation of New Englanders and became the stereotype of witches in later books and films: an elderly or indigent woman who earns a living by gathering herbs and mixing potions, who often in an earlier life was a midwife or simply had a long history of providing medicines and care to a small community. Such women were tolerated and, some would say, even more of a need than a nuisance in Puritan New England.

If a known witch's longstanding reputation took a bad turn, however, and she, besides, became haughty and insolent in response to a community's accusations, citizens turned against her with all manner of accusations based on long-held superstitions. Legends of witches permeated the New England landscape, especially those who held the power of shapeshifting, often appearing as cats, goats, crows or other birds in an effort to disguise their presence. Hence the legend of Granny Mott of Westerly, Rhode Island.

The small colony seemed to have a preponderance of witches, perhaps because of the longstanding tolerance of worship of one's own beliefs, no matter how far they fell outside the Puritan norm. It is a fact that while the Massachusetts Bay Colony, Connecticut and New Haven executed thirty-five

Illustration of the "witch panic." *Courtesy of Wikimedia Commons.*

men and women for witchcraft between 1642 and 1692,[22] not one woman or man was hanged for witchcraft in Rhode Island.

By the eighteenth century, according to a Rhode Island historian, a coven of witches was regularly gathering on a granite outcrop outside of Wickford, where they "held their unhallowed sabbaths in Hell Hollow and Kettle Hole."[23] One local historian has noted seventeen women in the same era who were presumed to be witches in the small town of Foster alone.[24]

In Newport, Baptist minister Ezra Stiles commented in his *Diary* on the relics of these "Almanack Makers and Fortune tellers…as old Granny Morgan at 70 now living in Newport accustoms herself on occasion to a hocus pocus, & making cakes of flour and her own Urine and sticking them full of pins and divining by them."[25]

Stiles also knew of a Mr. Stafford in Tiverton, Rhode Island, who, people professed, had the power to advise locals on "what day, hour and minute was fortunate for vessels to sail" and wrote as well of some midwives who commonly indulged in fortune telling.

The witchlike activities of Granny Mott first appeared in the Reverend S.S. Griswold's *Historical Sketch of the Town of Hopkington from 1757 to 1876.*

According to Griswold, Granny was a familiar, if not unnerving, sight to townspeople when their travels caused them to ride by the shack where she lived, close by the Pawcatuck River. She dressed in ragged clothes, her balding head was covered by thin strands of silver hair and her face, with its long, hooked nose, had grown cragged with age. She sold corncob charms to households, said to ward off evil spells. In her travels, she was always accompanied by a five-legged black cat.

When the river froze, the pair glided across the ice to the Connecticut shore and back, Granny singing in a high, screechy voice, and those who had resisted buying her charms would find their potatoes had frozen the next day or crockery had fallen from a shelf. On one occasion, a woman was left without speech for thirty-six hours.

In October 1750, the Potter family moved to the town and soon received a visit from Granny Mott, eager to sell her charms. She became a frequent

The Connecticut side of the Pawcatuck River, looking back at Westerly, Rhode Island. *Photo by author.*

visitor to the house, and during one visit, the Potter children, having heard she was a witch, determined to find out once and for all and set an upright awl in the seat of a chair offered to her. When the old woman sat down for hours without any indication of pain, the children knew this confirmed their and others' suspicions.

When their father, Thomas Potter, arrived home, he angrily ordered Granny Mott from the house and admonished his children for their foolishness. The old woman was seen shaking her fist at the household as she headed down the road.

The following day brought cooling temperatures, and around dusk, Thomas Potter ordered his children outside to help pick the last batch of fruit before a frost. As the children collected berries, a heath hen circled and swooped down at them.[26] Normally a docile bird, this hen plunged down again at the baskets, beating its wings against the face of one child. Potter told the children to go inside and collected his musket, fitting a silver coin into the barrel. When the hen circled again, he fired, and it fell to the ground dead.

That night, the river froze, and those who expected to hear Granny Mott's hideous song as she traversed the Pawcatuck were surprised when a silent night passed to daybreak. A child walking past Granny's shack that morning noticed her five-legged cat staring intently into the thin sheet of ice on the river. Those later brought to the scene recognized the form of Granny Mott beneath the ice, and in the center of her forehead, a glint of silver shone from the coin Thomas Potter had fired the previous day.[27]

It is recorded in the town records of the day that on that night, "Thos. Potter Killd a witch."

Hopkington was, according to the Reverend Griswold, a dark portal for paranormal activity in the eighteenth century:

> *Many houses in Hopkington were haunted by spirits from the other world....Deep, strange noises were heard, lights of various hues were seen, windows were illuminated....Moaning cries were heard in the air, and many significant warnings of death were given; and maidens practiced various incantations in order to discover who their lovers and future husbands were to be.*[28]

Griswold's book contained a warning to those young ladies who were introduced in these years to traditions far removed from New England's Puritan shores but increasingly introduced into the colonies with the folkloric traditions and beliefs brought by both enslaved and free individuals from many continents.

The minister tells of two girls, Hanna Maxson and Comfort Cottrell of Westerly, Rhode Island, who were guests at the home of Elisha Clarke, Esq., during the time of the Revolutionary War. Clarke had married Mary Potter in 1743 and was a veteran of the French and Indian War. Their four children would have been grown and moved on by the time of the Revolution, when Clarke was approaching sixty. Hanna was the niece of Mary Potter, daughter of Martha Potter Maxson. Her brother Matthew Maxson Jr. served as a private during the war and would marry Frances Fanny Peckham in February 1778.

Town well in Norwich, Connecticut. *Photo by author.*

Perhaps it was this event that, the following summer, set Hanna and her friend on their efforts of divining who their future husbands might be. They cast balls of yarn into Elisha Clarke's well and rewound them while reciting the Scriptures backward as dusk fell about the yard.

According to Griswold's account, it wasn't long before a monstrous form appeared from the edge of the darkness. In their panicked flight down the path back to the house, the girls swore that the creature breathed fire and had enormous eyes.

They entered the house and bolted the door, screaming in terror as they fled to the bedroom of Hanna's aunt, who lay in bed recuperating from illness. Their cries brought an impatient Elisha Clarke to the room, who soon heard the tale these two vain and immature young woman had to impart: namely that, in their careless incantations, they had invited Satan to be their groom.

Clarke retrieved the family Bible and went to the front door to confront the creature. According to Griswold, the elder could see the creature's glowing eyes through the transom window above the bolted door. Undaunted, he prayed aloud until the creature was gone.

Such superstitions concerning spells and the suspicions that fell on elderly women continued well into the era of Enlightenment. When a group of former enslaved workers in Concord, Massachusetts, established a free community along the edge of Walden Woods, "so fearsome became the reputation of the area that anxious travelers raced through it as fast as they could."[29] One of the community's best-known residents was an elderly Black woman named Zilpah White. Occupying a small house on the corner of a thoroughfare, she often startled passersby with her "shrill singing" and loud cackling over her stewpot. "Ye are all bones, bones," she was reputed to have called out in glee. Remaining fiercely independent to the end, even as she suffered from near blindness, Zilpah White died at the age of seventy-two in 1820.

Perhaps perceived as more of a threat to the community's moral authority were those young woman, and often men as well, who purposely spent much of their day in leisure activities, drank wine or spirits liberally and were, on occasion, witnessed exhibiting lewd behavior while in public. In all such practices, the hand of the devil was seen to be orchestrating the lives of those individuals who allowed him to possess them. Worse still, such behavior lured others to stray from their lives of constrained piousness to ones that contested authority and allowed such selfish pleasures to ruin their reputations.

While many readers are likely aware of the hysteria that later gripped Salem, Massachusetts, and led to the infamous witch trials of 1692, some may be surprised to learn that the colony of Connecticut hanged seven women and two men convicted of practicing witchcraft between 1647 and 1663.

Two of these convicted were husband and wife Nathaniel and Rebecca Greensmith of Hartford, Connecticut. In 1662, they became the unwitting victims of a growing hysteria in the colony.

When the eight-year-old daughter of their neighbor John Kelly fell ill in the spring of that year, she allegedly called out in her fevered delirium that a neighbor had laid the affliction on her. When she expired, family and friends began to suspect that this bewitchment had been the cause of her demise. Around the same period, a young girl named Ann Cole, also of Hartford, began to suffer strange fits, during which, it was believed, the devil himself spoke through her.

The girl was carefully examined by four local ministers, and suspicion soon loomed over a family considered troublesome by most in the community.

Nathaniel and Rebecca Greensmith lived on twenty acres in Hartford County with a house and barn. Two of three daughters from Rebecca's previous marriage, now seventeen and fifteen, completed the family. The

Greensmiths were judged harshly by the community, as Nathaniel soon gained a reputation as a thief and a liar in court. His wife, especially as she was a widow, was frowned on for the company she kept, being that of other ill-thought-of women, often suspected of adultery and fornication, and she was observed dancing and drinking wine beneath a tree on the common, a site that was also allegedly used for nocturnal gatherings by the same women.

As with most cases, a formal charge of witchcraft began the well-known process of interviewers pitting neighbor against neighbor until a bounty of complaints and ill luck that had occurred was compiled for examination of the accused pair.

The Greensmiths were arrested and brought before the court on December 30, 1662. While in prison, Rebecca was interviewed by the Reverends Hayes and Whiting. Their account of her confession reads, in part: "She [Rebecca] forthwith and freely confirms these things to be true, that she [and other prisoners named...] had familiarity with the devil."[30]

Asked if she had pledged covenant with the devil, Rebecca denied having done so, only admitting that "she promised to go with him when he comes (which she had accordingly done several times) but that the devil told her that at Christmas they would have a merry meeting and then the covenant should be done and subscribed."[31]

Rebecca also told the ministers that the devil

> *first appeared to her in the form of a deer or fawn, skipping about her, wherewith she was not much affrightened but by degrees he contrived to talk with her, and that their meetings were frequently at such a place (near her own house) that some of the company came in one shape and some in another, and one in particular in the shape of a crow came flying to them.*[32]

She also informed the spellbound clergymen that the devil "had frequent use of her body."[33]

Such a confession would most likely be laughable in today's court proceedings and the defendant required to undergo a psychological examination. But in colonial New England, such tales were taken in all seriousness. The two ministers described Rebecca Greensmith in their report as "lewd, ignorant" and, despite being only in her late thirties, "a considerably aged woman."[34]

In court the following January, Rebecca indicted her husband as being a pawn of the devil as well, citing several occasions when, while looking for stray livestock in the forest, she witnessed once a "red creature" and, on another occasion, two creatures "like dogs, one a little blacker than ye other" came close to her husband and seemed familiar with him.

Rebecca also named neighbors such as Goody Seager and Goodwives Ayers and Sandford as having taken part in meetings with her and said that those nocturnal gatherings also included James Walkely, Peter Grant's wife and Henry Palmer's wife from Wethersfield.

After Rebecca Greensmith's testimony, the couple was sentenced to death and, January 1662, hanged on Gallows Hill, a bluff just north of where Trinity College stands. The site "afforded an excellent view of the execution to a large crowd on the meadows to the west, a hanging being then a popular spectacle and entertainment."[35]

Another among the accused in Hartford managed to flee to Rhode Island after her third trial in Connecticut. Elizabeth Seager had been indicted for blasphemy, adultery and witchcraft in previous trials. In this last deposition filed against her, Elizabeth faced charges from her neighbor Goodwife Margaret Garrett that her witchcraft had caused Goodwife Garrett's block of cheese to become ridden with maggots.

When she was found guilty in June 1665, Elizabeth Seager may well have expected to be hanged, but a finding of the court of assistants that the jury's

Early woodcut of witch hangings, 1655. *Attributed to Richard Gardiner in "England's Grievance Discovered."*

verdict did not legally answer to the indictment set her "free from further suffering or imprisonment."

While free from prison, she soon suffered the wrath of neighbors who were outraged that she had escaped the hanging. After having spent a year in prison, Elizabeth Seager quickly left her Connecticut home behind and "found Rhode Island a more congenial place of residence."[36]

The witch hysteria only grew throughout the region in the years following. While it has become the town of Salem's lot to be known as the "witch capital" of New England, when Governor Sir William Phips appointed nine Boston judges to form a court for hearings in May 1692, "the jails of Salem, Ipswich, other North Shore towns, and Boston were overflowing with suspected witches."[37]

The most prominent of the witch trial judges, Samuel Sewall alone took the "blame and shame" for the twenty women and men executed and the ten more women found guilty of witchcraft during the hysteria. In 1697, he stood before the congregation of the Third Church of Boston and publicly repented. In later writings, he would reflect on the steadfastness of Puritan ideology that led to that summer of injustice: "Men think 'tis a disgrace to change their mind…but there is not a greater folly than not to give place to right reason."[38]

In 2022, some of the descendants of those convicted of witchcraft in Connecticut petitioned the state to declare the eleven women and men wrongfully convicted and officially pardon them. Though meeting resistance from town officials who note that current law does not "offer pardons to people who are already dead," a group of activists calling themselves CT Witch Memorial has steadfastly been gaining ground on having Connecticut's pardon law changed so that their ancestors may receive justice.

INDIGENOUS AMERICANS AND ENGLISH JUSTICE

Beyond the prevailing fear of the devil in New England was an almost equal fear of its Indigenous people. In that respect, what is perhaps most striking in Connecticut's code of law are the list of rules and regulations pertaining to the Indigenous peoples of the region. Property being a longstanding misunderstanding between Indigenous and White signers of treaties meant that those Indigenous people who came back, as was customary, to spend time in their ancestral lands were now regarded as trespassers:

It is ordered and decreed that where any company of Indians doe sitt downe
neare any English Plantations, that they shall declare whoe is their Sachem
or Chiefe, and that the said Sachem or Chiefe shall pay to the said English
such trespasses as shall be committed by any Indian in the said plantation
adjoining, either by spoyling or killing any Cattle or Swyne, either with
trapps, dogs, or arrows.[39]

It must be noted that the English often let their cattle and swine roam freely, and it was these that were getting trapped and killed when the Indigenous people came around with their dogs to check the traps they had set in the forest and alongside brooks and streams.

Fines were established for a variety of offenses, both suspect and real: theft, damage to property and especially citizens, as indicated in this warning to the court:

Forinasmuch as [our] *lenity or gentines towards Indians have made them*
growe bold and insolent, to enter into Englishmens howses, and unadvisedly
handle swords and peeces and other instruments, many times to the hazard
of limbs of English or Indians…it is ordered, that whatsoever Indian shall
hereafter meddle with or handle any Englishmans weapons, of any sorte,
either in their howses or fields, they shall forfeit for every defaulte half a
fathom of wampum; and if any hurte or injury shall thereupon follow to
any persons life or limbe, wound for wound, and shall pay for the healing
of such wounds and other damages.

Foremost in mind was the fear of uprising. The troubled years leading up to the Pequot War and its dark legacy in New England still loomed like a shadow over the prospects of peaceful settlement. All the colonies in early New England established laws against selling firearms, powder and any weaponry to Indigenous peoples within the first years of settlement.

Trade for firearms and ammunition had produced a slew of early Dutch and English traders in the hustling early years of settlement. Perhaps with that in mind, Connecticut's law included a way to lower the number of guns in the Indigenous community, forbidding blacksmiths or any skilled settlers to "amend, repair, or cause to bee amended or repaired any gunn, small or great, belonging to any Indian, nor shall endeavor the same."[40]

The law further forbade settlers to sell the Indigenous peoples any dogs or weapons they might use for hunting or trade with them in any fashion. An early phenomenon of English settlers adapting Indigenous ways of living and even "joining" tribes by adoption or marriage to an Indigenous bride also became a focus of the law in the colonies. Connecticut levied perhaps the strictest punishment for the abandonment of English society, declaring,

> *Whereas divers persons departe from amongst us, and take up abode with the Indians, in a profane course of life, for the preventing thereof, it is ordered that whatsoever persons that now inhabiteth, or shall inhabit within this jurisdiction, and shall departe from us and settle or joine with the indians, that they shall suffer three years imprisonment at least. In the Howse of Correction.*[41]

Indigenous people, and later the enslaved men of color who would labor on the newly established farms or in the towns, were immediately suspected of robbery, rape and other violence against women and settlers.

One current historian argues, "Capital punishment was intrinsically entwined with class and race in early urban North America....The lower classes, both free and bound, bore the brunt of the hangman's noose. Laborers, sailors, servants, slaves, transients and young adults were the most vulnerable."[42]

The first hanging in Connecticut was of an Indigenous man named Nepauduck who had been convicted of murder. He was publicly hanged in New Haven on January 30, 1639.

The Massachusetts Bay Colony attempted to include Indigenous peoples into its systems of law, trying several early cases where punishment was meted out to Euro-Americans who had committed wrongs against local Indians.[43] In October 1631, Governor John Winthrop recorded having received a letter from "Captain Wiggin," the agent or overseer of the upper colony. The letter informed Winthrop of "a murder committed the 3rd of this month at Richman's Isle, by an Indian Sagamore called Squidrayset, and his company, upon one Walter Bagnall, called Great Watt."[44]

The agent sought advice as to whether they should raise a militia to pursue the accused but thought there might be others already in pursuit and with winter coming on…etcetera. Those who committed the murder were never captured. Winthrop wrote what might have been the deciding factor in letting the Indigenous people serve their own justice: "This Bagnall was sometimes servant to one in the Bay, and these three years had dwelt alone in the said Isle, and had gotten about £400 in goods. He was a wicked fellow, and had much wronged the Indians."[45]

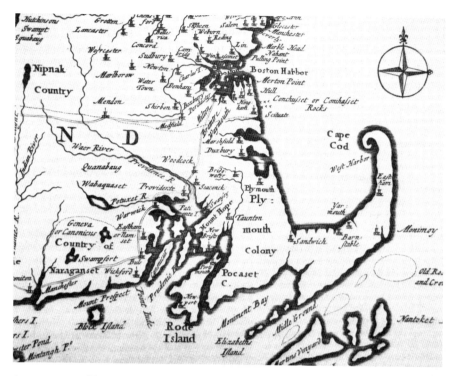

An exact map of New England and New York, London, 1702. *Published in Mather's* Magnalia Christi Americana.

In 1638, another incident occurred when four servants from Plymouth ran away from their masters and headed down the main route to Providence. There, they robbed and mortally wounded an Indigenous man, who escaped and lived long enough to alert other Indians to the crime before he expired. Learning that the crime had been reported, three of the prisoners fled and were captured shortly after on Aquidneck Island.

The governor recorded,

> *The three prisoners, being brought to Plymouth, and there examined, did all confess the murder, and that they did it to get his wampum, etc. but all the question was about the death of the Indian, for no man could witness that he saw him dead. But Mr. Williams and Mr. James of Providence made oath, that his wound was mortal, etc. At last two Indians, who, with much difficulty, were procured to come to the trial, (for they still feared that the English were conspired to kill all Indians) made oath after this manner... upon this they three were condemned and executed.*[46]

Nineteenth-century photo of Newport Courthouse. *Author's collection.*

A fourth had escaped but was captured by the local tribe and taken away for them to impart their own justice.

The records of the early General Court of Tryalls show that Rhode Island also took early steps to prevent the sale of liquor, guns and powder to Indigenous peoples. These early records also show the colony's uneasy interaction with Indigenous people, many of whom were hired as laborers in the towns and villages but were always suspect; some even mocked the perpetual fear the White settlers seemed to possess even as they hired them to build walls, burn their fields and perform menial labor within the town itself.

As Indigenous laborers and servants became integrated into the communities of the colony, the same development of the townspeople's suspicions and the mocking of those fears in a quasi-violent fashion began to emerge in the courts. One later case from the town of Newport provides an example.

On June 15, 1671, in the Newport Court of Tryalls, an Indigenous laborer named John by the English but know by his people as Quashcome was indicted "for offering very great abussis [abuses] unto Martha the wife of Edward Lay by throwing her downe in the high way and acting as if he would Ravish her &c."[47]

The defendant declared to the court that he could not recall if he had committed the act or not, as he was drunk on the occasion. The judges of the court soon declared him guilty of these acts "of a very heinous nature" but faced a dilemma. As the colony had yet to enact the death penalty for any offense but the crime of murder, those judges felt compelled to tell the general assembly, "Wee are fully satisfied that he is worthy of Death, and are ffree that Sentence of Death to be past on said prisoner."[48]

The assembly did not agree and asked the court to find another "exemplary punishment."

In May 1672, another case appeared before the court, an indictment against an Indigenous man simply named William, "for Entering the house of John Oldin of Newport and there in a violent manner did bite and wound the servant of the said Oldin."[49]

The defendant pled guilty and was sentenced to pay Oldin eleven pounds "in Consideration of his loss charge and Expense" as well as twenty shillings in court fees. The court then ordered that

> the said Indian be kept in safe custody until he pay the said sums or otherwise give good security for it, which if he does not performe within three months then that the said Indian be sold as a slave by the Treasure[r] to Barbados or Else where by the first oppertunety.[50]

On May 23, 1673, the General Court of Trials convicted an Indigenous man named Punneane for the "rape and murder of Lettice Bulger, wife of Richard of Portsmouth." He was sentenced to death by hanging and executed on May 23, 1673, in a public hanging held around one o'clock in the afternoon.

The following year, the attorney general brought an indictment against one Awassnew, "an Indian for murtheringe an Indian," though the accused never appeared in court. That same session brought another indictment against an elderly Native American named Quaoganit "for Murtheringe his wife and another Indian in the Month of March last past."[51]

The accused pled guilty to the crime, and the court wrote out its grim sentence:

> The Court doe centance the said Indian called old man to be carried from hence to the common Gaole and there strictly secured, and on the 19th day of this instant month to be carried to the place of Execution, the Gallows, and there be hanged by the neck until he be dead dead.[52]

CHAPTER 2

EARLY CASES OF MURDER AND THE PASSION FOR PUBLIC EXECUTIONS

T he reader might be curious as to the need to emphasize the certain expiration of the convicted man or woman. In early New England, the act of hanging an individual was performed with the use of a cart, a strong rope and the suitable limb of a tree, whether it be outside or inside the town or village. The convicted would be "drawn up" in the cart to the place of execution and made to stand while the rope was draped over the limb. A suitably strong man held the end of the rope while the noose was placed around the convicted man or woman's neck. With a shouted order, the cart was pulled forward and left the prisoner dangling; the length of time it took to kill the convicted depended on the strength of the man holding the rope and the limb that supported it.

There were, early on, occasions where the convicted did not die due to a premature end to the proceedings, as in the case of a broken limb or a rope that failed before the convicted expired. For a time, those who survived an initial hanging were strung up again, until protest against the practice led to laws that permitted the release of a prisoner should they survive an attempted execution by the state.

Gallows were a later innovation and almost exclusively used after 1700. It became customary for the General Court of Tryalls to order that a gallows be built for an execution and then taken down after the spectacle of the hanging was over.

Early Cases of Murder

In September 1639, the town of Salem, Massachusetts, brought one Marmaduke Percy before the court of assistants and arraigned him on charges of murder for the death of his apprentice. An inquest had found sufficient evidence to forward the bill for murder, but "the jury of life and death could not agree" and the case was moved up to the next quarterly court. The defendant was allowed to go free on bail.

This may have given Percy time to rally his neighbors against what appears to have been a child apprentice who was disliked by more than one in the community. When Percy was brought again before the court in December, these friends and neighbors were there with him. As Winthrop recorded,

> *The jury being called, had further evidence given them, which tended to the clearing of Percy; yet two of the jury dissented from the rest, who were all agreed to acquit him. In the end it had this issue, that these two were silent, and so the verdict was received.*
>
> *The cause was this: The boy was ill disposed, and his master gave him unreasonable correction, and used him ill in his diet. After, the boy gate [got] a bruise on his head, so as there appeared a fracture in his skull, being dissected after his death.*
>
> *Now, two things were in the evidence, which made the case doubtful; one, the boy his charging his master, before his death, to have given him that wound with his meatyard and with a broomstaff (for he spake of both at several times;) the other was, that he had told another, that his hurt came with the fall of a bough from a tree; and other evidence there was none.*[53]

The first murder of a White man in Providence, Rhode Island, in 1660 was allegedly committed by an Indigenous man, though many in town assumed he had been hired by a contentious neighbor intent on obtaining a parcel of the murdered man's lands. The case against the Indigenous man never made it to trial. He was placed under guard at the Mowry Tavern while shackles were made by a blacksmith, and his testimony in the inquiry that followed caused the town to order the shackled man to Newport in the custody of an appointed deputy who would row him from the mainland across the wintry bay to the island for trial. As records indicate, the boat never arrived. Providence then decided it needed a jail to hold prisoners, if necessary, until the spring.[54]

A decade later, Kings County executed the first White person to be convicted of murder within its jurisdiction. On July 11, 1670, the attorney general indicted Thomas Flounders of Kings County for the murder of his neighbor and nemesis Walter House. The two had been arguing over land for some years, and House may have taken Flounders to court concerning their dispute several months before but never showed to testify on his complaint. By mid-July, on the occasion of House visiting Flounders's shop on the Post Road, a heated argument escalated into a physical confrontation, and House was left dead.[55] Moreover, Flounders hastily buried the body to cover up his act, and on July 13, the court ordered that the body be "unearthed and an inquest be made."[56]

At his examination two days later, Flounders admitted to the killing but claimed self-defense, saying he had hit House with a stick, causing him to fall backward and hit his head, which caused his fatal injury. On inspecting the body, however, the jury of men observed multiple bruises and contusions and could only determine that Flounders had beaten Walter House to death. The court's sentence reflects the indignation of its jurors:

> *The Judgement of the Court is unaminously That hee suffer death as the Law hath provided in Such Casses which is to be hanged until his body be dead which sentence is to be Excicuted on wensday being the 2 Day of November between the owre of nine in the morning and two in the afternone.*[57]

On the docket of the General Court of Trials in May 1673 was the case of Thomas Cornell, accused of murdering his mother, Rebecca, in the family's home on the one-hundred-acre farm they owned on West Main Road in Portsmouth, Rhode Island.

Cornell was a fairly prominent person in the town. His father had been a hero in the Indian wars of the previous generation, and Cornell Jr. himself had been elected deputy to the general assembly and served as a juror on several important cases presented before the General Court of Tryalls. Cornell was a widower, and he, along with his second wife, Sarah, four sons from his previous marriage and two daughters from the present marriage, as well as his seventy-three-year-old mother and two male boarders, made up the household.

Like many Rhode Island landowners in the seventeenth century, Cornell owned livestock including oxen, cattle, a large herd of sheep and horses that he raised for the local market. Then, as now, those who earn a living from the land spent long days working out of doors, especially in the throes of winter.

On his return to the house on February 8, 1673, Cornell learned that his mother was unwell and, visiting her room, found his son Thomas Jr. sitting

Thomas Cornell house. *Courtesy of the Portsmouth, Rhode Island Historical Society.*

with her. Father and son sat and talked with Rebecca until darkness fell. Thomas Jr. left the room, and his father remained. Around seven o'clock, Cornell left his mother to tend to the task of spinning some yarn, and when that was finished, he sat down at the table with his family for a dinner of "salt-mackrill."

Rebecca had declined to join them, but as the meal ended, Sarah asked her stepson Edward to go to his grandmother's room and inquire as to whether she would like some boiled milk—a common digestive for those with weak stomachs at the time—brought up to her. It had been perhaps an hour since the elder Thomas had left her alone in the chamber.

According to Edward's later testimony, he called out to his grandmother on opening the door to her room. Receiving no response, he entered the room, spied flames and then rushed back out to alert the household.

Boarder Henry Straite was the first to reach the room. He "clapped his hands" on the fire consuming the huddled form. In the confusion, Straite believed the darkened form to be an Indigenous man who had broken into the house while intoxicated and inadvertently set himself on fire. As improbable as that may seem, the fear of Indigenous people and their "mischief" was very prevalent at that time.

Once the flames were extinguished, it took only moments to realize that the victim was Rebecca Cornell. Someone in the household was immediately dispatched to summon the neighbors as well as William Baulston, the town coroner. Well into the night, men from neighboring houses came to view the grisly scene. When the last departed, a family member would have sat all night with the body as it lay, partially burned, on the floor.

Baulston arrived on Sunday morning and hastily convened a twelve-man jury of inquest, several members of which had viewed the body the night before and found the victim to be "very much scorched & burdnt by fire."[58]

The jury's judgment, after examining and "handling" the body, was that Rebecca Cornell was "brought to her untimely death by an unhappie accident of fire as shee sat in her rome."[59]

This kind of "unhappie accident" was not unknown to families in early New England; skirts and aprons easily caught fire from the fireplace in the process of cooking or even placing a kettle on the fire. A cautious woman sewed a hem of wool at the bottom of her skirt or apron to alert her by smell if it caught fire as well as to slow the flames.

Here the case would most likely have ended but for a strange occurrence that happened to John Briggs, the brother of Rebecca Cornell. Two nights after his sister's death, as he

> *"lay in his bedd…being between sleeping and wakeing" he opened his eyes, sensing something in the room, and saw "a light in the rome, like the dawning of the day, and plainly saw the shape and appearance of a woman standing by his bedside."*[60]

Briggs cried out in fright, but the apparition spoke to him and told him that she was his sister, twice asking, "See how I am burdnt with fire?" Rebecca's brother also testified that that apparition seemed badly burned, "about the shoulders, face and head."

In the aftermath of the revelation of Briggs's visitation, the town of Portsmouth was stirred into a whirlwind of rumor and speculation. While the apparition did not blame anyone for her death or speak of murder, the appearance of a spirit was often believed to indicate a wronged soul seeking justice, and it raised suspicion that the death of Rebecca Cornell was no mere accident.

Ten days after the funeral, Rebecca's body was exhumed and reexamined. Two professional surgeons were engaged to conduct the autopsy. Their findings included a previously unnoticed wound to the stomach, caused, in

An iron spindle. *Courtesy of Smith's Castle historic house museum.*

their estimation, by "some instrument licke, or the iron spyndell of a spinning whelle."[61]

Suspicion soon fell on Thomas Cornell. It was well known in town that an unbridled animosity had grown in recent years between Rebecca and her eldest son. Though the house was his to inherit, Rebecca still managed the property as well as the remainder of her late husband's estate. While Thomas had to take a bond from his mother to improve their dwelling, Rebecca gave away large tracts of valuable land in New York to his sisters and their husbands. There seems also to have been a dispute between Thomas and his brother, as they collectively sued to remove the son from the homestead.

Thomas had fallen into debt and owed his mother and her estate some £200 at the time of her death. Neighbors felt obliged to report the times he had spoken ill of his mother. He had, at times, called her cruel and even accused her of witchcraft.

Cornell was arrested and tried in the meetinghouse where he had often served as a juror. Attorney General John Easton indicted the accused by presenting the case that "the sayd Thomas Cornell did violently Kill his Mother, Rebeca Cornell, Widdow, or was adying or Abetting thereto, in the Dwelling House of his sayd Mother."[62]

He was found guilty of the charge and sentenced that on "the 23rd Day of this instant month May, about One of the Clocke, to be carryd from the sayd Gaole to the place of Execution, the Gallows, and there to be hanged by ye neck until you are Dead Dead."[63] Cornell was hanged in the Courthouse Square of Newport before a large crowd.

Connecticut's code of law was challenged in 1712 by the case of murder brought before the New London court against a father and son, John and Daniel Gard, accused of killing William Whitear, a visitor from Long Island.

The Gards had gone to visit their longtime acquaintance, a Stonington sea captain named Daniel Eldridge. Whitear was a guest at the house. At some point, an argument broke out between Whitear and Daniel Gard, who challenged the visitor to a fight outside. As the incident was recorded in the court records,

On the 16th day of August 1712, a quarrel arose at the house of Daniel Eldrige in Stonington, between the prisoner Daniel Gard, and William Whitear, a stranger, and that the said prisoner challenged Whitear to fight; whereupon they went out of the house and closed in on one another, and that the said prisoner threw Whitear on the ground and fell with him, and there lay until they were parted; and that said. Whitear said he told the prisoner immediately that he had killed him.[64]

The victim's words were prophetic. Seven days after the fight, he expired. An autopsy found that his bladder, injured in the fight, had burst and his death was caused by the resultant infection.

A long infamous case in the colony of Rhode Island was the conviction of Thomas Carter of Newport for murdering trader William Jackson of Virginia in 1751. The crime began as a robbery on the Post Road as it ran through what was then called Kings County, a well-traveled route by both stagecoach and business travelers. The most detailed account lies in the memoirs of Wilkins Updike, Esq., grandson of Daniel Updike Jr., who, as attorney general, brought the case before the jury.

Carter owned a small vessel, of which he went Master, and sailed from Newport where he resided, to New York. He was wrecked on Long Island, and lost all, and borrowed money to defray the expense of his return. He landed on the Connecticut shore, and in his journey home, on foot, he fell in company with Mr. Jackson, a Virginian, bound for Newport, drawing a horse laden with dressed deer skins, for sale, and the proceeds to be invested in Narragansett horses for the home market.[65]

Jackson must have been a sight to Carter, dressed in leather shirt and breeches, with a snuff-colored jacket and "red duffel over coat." He carried a saw-backed hanger (the equivalent of today's bowie knife) at his side along with a leather purse and a gold watch with a green ribbon for a chain.

Updike writes that "both being destined for the same place, they traveled together, passing New London late at night. On the 31st December 1750, they arrived at South Kingstown, and tarried at Nathanial Nash's."

The following morning, Carter complained of feeling ill. Despite his eagerness to reach Newport before nightfall, Jackson relented and let Carter convalesce until noon. While waiting, he had the innkeeper, Nash, cut his hair and give him a shave. The innkeeper's wife repaired his overcoat with

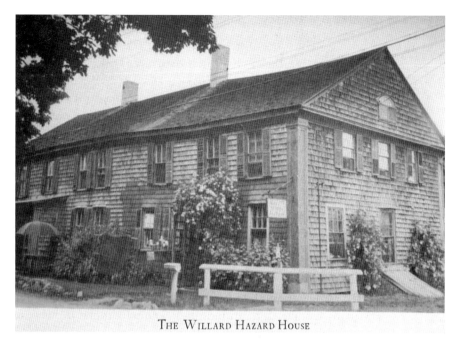

THE WILLARD HAZARD HOUSE

Willard Hazard house, once Nash's tavern. *Courtesy of the Ponaganset Historical Society.*

some new buttons, noticing the monogrammed linen and his heavy purse, which, she would later estimate, weighed five or six pounds.

> *In the afternoon they left, Carter procrastinated the journey by stopping at every shop and tavern on the way, and calling for liquor freely, until evening, assuring Jackson that there was enough time to reach the ferry, and take the earliest boat for Newport, in the morning. When passing the hill above where the Quaker Meeting house now stands* [roughly the intersection of today's Routes 1 and 138], *Carter stated it was too late to reach the ferry before all were abed, and no admission could be obtained, and persuaded him to remain in an untenanted house by the road.*

Jackson again relented to Carter's wishes, though as the night progressed, he grew increasingly uneasy and pressed Carter to resume their journey to the ferry-house. Carter attempted to deflect his growing suspicion, but Jackson "insisted upon proceeding and when they left the house, Carter struck him with a stone, and felled him to the ground. Jackson begged for life, but Carter seized Jackson's hanger, and dispatched him."

After riffling through his victim's clothes and securing his leather purse and watch, Carter "took the dead body, weltering in blood, on his shoulder, and carried it near a mile, and deposited it under the ice, in the southern arm of the Patasquamscut River, and in cutting the hole he broke the hanger."[66]

Carter returned to the abandoned house, hid Jackson's bloodied overcoat in a wall and then took his horse and proceeded to the ferry-house.

Carter apparently had a restless night with the certainty that he had left behind some incriminating evidence, for he returned to the house again the next morning and happened on one Jonathan Hazard, who had his dogs out hunting. The hounds soon scented blood and led Hazard to the abandoned house and scene of the crime.

When the hunter questioned Carter about the blood, the murderer evaded his questions and demanded, in a threatening manner, that he call off his dogs. Such was Carter's temperament, Hazard would later testify, that he feared for his own safety and relented to Carter's demand.

Carter hurried on to Newport after this encounter, inquiring along the way if any fellow travelers had heard any "news from Narragansett."

"The Narrows" on the southern end of the Pettaquamscutt River. *Photo by author.*

The body of William Jackson was discovered by ice fishermen about seven weeks after the murder, on the twenty-second of February 1751. Carter was arrested the next day in Newport, never having made any effort to escape and keeping in his possession several of the deerskins, the monogrammed linen and the watch chain ribbon.

In total, twenty-seven witnesses were interviewed about their observations and interactions with Carter before and after the crime. All testified against the accused. Despite the fact that, throughout the trial, the defendant expressed little remorse or emotion, this changed on the day of his sentencing when the judge added on to the sentence of death the indignity "that the body of the executed shall be hung in chains."[67]

"For this," Updike wrote, "he was not prepared, and when it was announced from the bench, he lost all self-possession—became entirely unnerved, and cried out for mercy from the gibbet."[68]

As written in the sentence handed down, the convicted man was

> *to be drawn to the place of execution, and there Between the Hours of Eleven o'clock forenoon and two o'clock in the afternoon to be hung by the Neck till you are Dead, and then your Body to be cut Down and Hanged in Chains over the place of Execution till Consumed.*[69]

Carter was hanged and the sentence enacted on the tenth of May 1751. His body hung for years in an iron gibbet at the intersection of the Post Road and the old Kingston Road. It became somewhat of a tourist attraction for travelers passing through.

Nearly four years after the execution, the Reverend Jacob Bailey, a recent graduate of the Harvard Divinity School, was traveling through the area with friends and spent the night at the popular tavern operated on Tower Hill by Squire Case. The tavern keeper told the party of the murder and offered to take them "down the hill to see the murderer hung in the gibbets." Bailey and his friends dutifully accompanied their host to the site, where, as Bailey recorded "we beheld the horrible sight. The man had been in there three years already, and his flesh was all dried fast to his bones."[70]

In numerous ways, public executions profited the community. These occasions became much advertised in newspapers and well attended, benefiting nearby inns, taverns and other hostelries as well as those who boarded, repaired and performed general maintenance of the horses, carriages and wagons brought into town for the occasion.

The executioner and others benefited personally, as illustrated in records relating to the aforementioned cases. A fee of two pounds was paid to the executioner for "hanging the Indian that killed his wife" and it was noted that another one pound and twenty shillings was still due "for the executing T.C. (Thomas Cornell) and the other Indian."[71]

Edward Marshall and two other men were paid "15 & silver" for "bringing the Indian that broke prison and committed the rape on R. Bulgar's wife." John Potter of Warwick was paid one pound, three shillings for "taking the Indian prisoner that was executed" in the same case, and rum was paid to the guard who had performed their duty at the dual executions of Cornell and Punneane.[72]

Thomas Hazard, keeper of the South Kingstown jail, petitioned the state for additional compensation for securing Thomas Carter. In addition, Joseph Hull was also compensated for securing the prisoner in Kings County Jail as well as meals for watch (while he watched the prisoner), and "taking May 10 $ constructing & transmitting the (body) to gibbet."[73]

While murders related to robbery and personal disputes within families or with neighbors were most common, one of the most prevalent crimes, tragically borne of poverty and the fear of public shaming, was infanticide.

THE TRAGEDY OF INFANTICIDE

The crime of murdering a newborn child has a dark history reaching back across Europe and North America for millennia. That such an unspeakable crime was brought into the religious settlements of New England should have been no surprise, but the inherent evil implicit in those early cases would color the public conception of the true nature and cause of most infanticide cases for decades to come.

The stigma associated with giving birth to a bastard child continued to thrive in stiff-collared New England communities well into the nineteenth century. There was little difference in the circumstances in which women found themselves or in the judgment rendered between the seventeenth-century Puritans or the public shaming given two hundred years later.

Barely different also were the punishments meted out to the men involved. While in the 1600s, a man convicted of impregnating a housemaid of his or another's household or any other young, unmarried woman of the village might be subjected to a public "whipping at the cart" and a fine, the woman

Entrance to meetinghouse, Swansea, Massachusetts. *Photo by author.*

who bore the child and the child itself were often marked for life. Faced with such consequences, some chose a desperate and despicable measure.

One of the first noted cases in the colonies involved a twenty-two-year-old servant girl named Mary Martin. Mary lived and worked in Casco Bay on Maine's southern coast with her father. When he returned to England, she had an affair with a married man. When the affair was discovered, she found employment with the Bourne family in Boston. Once there, however, she discovered that she was pregnant. Her loose-fitting clothes concealed her condition for a time, but neighbors grew suspicious.[74]

Mary's mistress, Hannah Bourne, dismissed any gossip brought to her, and Mary continued working for the Bournes even as she learned that they, too, were preparing to return to England and that she would be left behind without her mistress's protection or even a roof over her head.

Mary gave birth in secret in a back room of the house, and when the infant began to cry, she attempted to kill the child immediately. When kneeling on it did not work, she battered the infant and threw the body in her trunk, cleaning the blood from the floor and rising the next morning as though nothing had occurred.

When the Bournes left for England six days later, they had no suspicions about Mary. But no sooner had the Bournes boarded the ship when a local midwife confronted the girl and pried a confession from her. Though she told the midwife she had thrown the infant's body in the fire, she was suspected of lying yet again, and soon, the grisly discovery of her battered newborn in her trunk was made.

John Winthrop recorded that once in court, a surgeon testified that the newborn had suffered a fractured skull. The child's body was presented to the jury, and by a superstitious tradition, Mary was forced to touch the face of her dead child, "whereupon the blood came fresh into it."[75]

This was perceived as her guilt revealed and prompted her confession. She was sentenced to "hang on the gallows in the Square at Boston."[76]

Winthrop recorded the grim scene as the sentence, carried out, went horribly wrong, for "after she was turned off and hung a space, she spake and asked what they did mean to do. Then some stepped up and turned the knot of the rope backward, and then she soon died."[77]

One early case that roused the indignation of the public was that of Esther Rodgers. Born in Kittery, Maine, about 1680, Esther was removed to Newbury, Massachusetts, by the time she was thirteen years of age and served as an apprentice to one Joseph Woodridge, in whose home she resided.

The Woodridge family were religious observers of the Sabbath, while Esther did not attend church on a religious basis and was noticeably bored when obliged to do so. At the age of seventeen, she confessed to have fallen "into that foul Sin of Uncleanliness, suffering myself to be defiled by a *Negro* Lad living in the same house."[78]

When Esther learned she was pregnant, she hid the fact, continued her relationship with the father of the child and resolved to kill the child when it was born. When her pregnancy came to an end, she was unmoved by giving birth and kept to her plan. She confessed to having "stopped the breath of it"[79] and, after murdering the child, hid the body in her room until nightfall, when she crept out to bury the infant in the garden.

When Esther Rodgers left Newbury six months later, none were the wiser. She soon took up residence in a public tavern in Piscatagua, New Hampshire, where she gave herself up to "other wicked Company and Ways of Evil" for the next year.

On her return to Newbury, Esther found herself unable to return to the house where she had committed the crime and sought lodgings in the seedier section of the town, where she "took all opportunities to follow my

Old Ipswich
Jail, Ipswich,
Massachusetts.
Courtesy of
Wikimedia
Commons.

old trade of running out a nights, or entertaining Sinful Companions in a back room of the House."[80]

Finding herself pregnant again, she again tried to hide her condition, and when the time came to give birth, she walked out beyond the village to a field and squatted there until the infant had fallen free. Uncertain as to whether the child was dead or alive, she carried the body to the side of a nearby pond and covered it with snow and mud before returning home.

This time, however, the neighbors were suspicious. Though defiant when plied with questions, Esther Rodgers had little choice but to confess when the body of her newborn infant was found and brought before her.

Held in the Newbury prison for several weeks, Esther was then carried to Ipswich for trial. The court, under Justice Samuel Sewall, found her guilty of murder on July 15, 1701.

During her time awaiting her death in the Ipswich prison, Esther was visited by no fewer than seven ministers, each of whom claimed credit for her conversion and confession to the killing of her earlier child. The extraordinary confession that these men of the cloth recorded was duly printed in newspapers, and whether her conversion was real or invented, Esther Rodgers gave quite a last penitent performance on the day of her execution.

On July 31, she chose to forgo the cart that would bring her to the gallows and chose to walk the mile and more on foot, accompanied by several of the ministers who had recorded her confessions.

It was said she faltered once but ascended to the gallows "without stop or trembling."

Esther Rodgers proceeded to address the crowd, concluding, "O my dear Friends—Take Warning by me. Here I come to Dy, and if God be not Merciful to my Soul, I shall be undone to all Eternity."[81]

With a handkerchief covering her face and the noose about her neck, she cried out one last prayer before the trapdoor beneath her feet was tripped open.

An infamous case presented itself on the morning of August 11, 1739, in Portsmouth, New Hampshire, when the body of a female infant was discovered in one of the town wells. The authorities swiftly issued a warrant and searched for the mother of the murdered child.

Neighbors of twenty-seven-year-old widow Sarah Simpson immediately alerted authorities of their suspicion that she had recently been with child. The widow was soon arrested, despite her protests that she was not the mother of the child found. Instead, she led the constable to a place along the Piscataqua River where, after a brief excavation, the body of her own

Town well, Weston, Vermont. *Photo by author.*

stillborn infant was found. She was placed in jail while authorities continued their search for the mother of the infant found in the well.

Suspicion then fell on twenty-year-old Penelope Kenny, an Irish immigrant and servant to Dr. Joseph Franklin, a leading physician in the town. The young woman denied giving birth, but after careful examination by "four or five skillful women," it was determined that she had indeed given birth within the past week.

She was placed in prison and, for a time, continued to deny that she had delivered a child but finally relented after intense interrogation. On the day of Christmas Eve, she summoned the judges to her cell and confessed that she had given birth to a male child the previous Wednesday and, in her panic, placed the newborn in a tub in her master's basement, only to find it dead when she returned two days later.

She then led the judges and ministers to the same riverbank, where she exhumed the body of her child, not sixty feet from where Sarah Simpson had buried her own infant.

Both women were hanged on December 27, 1739, in front of a large gathering that had come to witness the first execution in the province of New Hampshire.[82]

There is no indication that the mother of the infant found in the well was ever located or brought to justice.

In another unfortunate instance, servant Sarah Bramble of New London, Connecticut, was indicted for the murder of her illegitimate child "on the day of its birth" in April 1752. She spent months in jail, defiant of authorities. A jury tried her in September of that year but could not reach a verdict. She was finally sentenced the following October, never giving authorities the name of the child's father and refusing to attend the sermon written for her execution. Sarah Bramble was hanged in New London, Connecticut, on November 21, 1753. Witness Joshua Hempstead would record in his journal,

> In the after [noon] I Rid up to the Cross Highway [above] Jno Bolles to See Sarah Bramble Executed for the Murdering her Bastard Child in march last was a yeare Since. She was hanged at 3 [o'] Clock. A Crowd of Spectators of all sexes and nations yt are among us from the neighboring Towns as well as this. Judged to be Ten Thousand.[83]

Small wonder, then, that so many women who might find themselves in a similar predicament became transient during the colonial period, moving from place to place, sometimes to stay with relatives, sometimes completely

Nineteenth-century illustration of a Puritan hanging of a convicted woman. *From Samuel Drake's* New England Legends and Folklore.

on their own, with little choice but to eke out a living from serving as a launderess, seamstress or teacher.

Such was the case with thirty-one-year-old Ruth Blay of Hawke, New Hampshire. Raised in a widowed family, the Blay children knew poverty and transience from early on—the family was "warned out" of South Hampton, New Hampshire, when Ruth was but fourteen years of age. They may have sought refuge in Chester, New Hampshire, at the home of the eldest married daughter.[84]

It was here that Ruth Blay developed the skills to acquire work as a teacher in a "dame" school, a school for girls that taught the rudiments of education and then concentrated on those "home" skills of sewing, needlecraft and what would later be called home economics.

Ruth Blay's career as a teacher offered minimal pay, and she often worked repairing and even making dresses, as she did during her time in Sandown, New Hampshire, and saved money as well by boarding with the Tilton and Collins families.

While teaching at Hawke, New Hampshire, Ruth Blay met the Reverend John Page, a well-educated and respected minister who supervised the education of students in the town. He may have developed an intimate relationship with Miss Blay, which resulted in her learning that she was pregnant in the fall of 1767.

As with many who faced this dilemma, Ruth Blay would bear the consequences with public humiliation once her condition became apparent and, worse still, the certainty of charges from the authorities and pressure to name the child's father in a court of law. Such prospects sent many women packing to other towns, where, if they were fortunate, they had relations who would take them in through the remainder of their pregnancies.

In colonial New England, even this was a risky act for the family that took in any relation from out of town. Landowners were often required to vouch for any person taken into their home for a period of time. Even then, magistrates kept a sharp eye on anyone who might become a dependent of the town. Drifters or persons simply seeking employment or a fresh start in a new location were under constant scrutiny. Many who had not found employment within thirty days or had no means by which to support themselves were "warned out" by authorities—that is, given a specified amount of time within which they were to leave town voluntarily, after which they could expect a forced expulsion.

Ruth Blay sought refuge with relations who lived in South Hampton, the Currier family, whose daughters were distant cousins. Phebe, the widow of

Reuben Currier, who had died in 1766, occupied one end of the large, five-bay Colonial house on Main Street, and her son Rueben Jr. and his wife, Elizabeth, occupied the other. Ruth's arrival at the household coincided with the birth of the couple's first child in May 1768. She likely helped the young mother with taking care of the infant as well as housekeeping and cooking before she herself gave birth on the night of June 10, 1768.

As revealed in her book on the tragedy, author Carolyn Marvin points out that when a woman became pregnant within the network of family and community, the ordeal was cushioned by a considerable amount of support, including midwives and housewives with old remedies for the onset of morning sickness the other difficulties of pregnancy, as well as childbirth itself.

But for outcasts like Ruth, "while it seems nearly impossible that some of the women of the house, as well as neighboring women, would not be aware of Ruth's pregnancy, as far as can be determined...she gave birth alone."[85]

The child was stillborn, likely caused, as Ruth later testified, by a couple of falls she had suffered recently and, she believed, brought on the birth itself.

As Marvin notes, "If she had produced but one witness to testify the child was stillborn, there would have been no suspicion of infanticide."

But in her panic, Ruth brought the infant's body to a barn belonging to Benjamin Clough, just over the border of the Currier property, and buried it there beneath some loose floorboards.

"This would give more credence," the historian says, "to the belief that she gave birth alone and hastily hid the body there, perhaps planning to bury it more properly when she had recovered from a difficult birth endured under such primitive conditions."[86]

Just four days later, however, some children of visitors to the property found the lifeless infant beneath the loose floorboards of the barn. An investigation was swiftly enacted, and that same day, the local justice of the peace sent a warrant to Isaac Brown, the constable of South Hampton, for the arrest of Ruth Blay.

The local coroner, to whom the infant's body had been turned over, convened a jury of sixteen men of the town to determine the infant's cause of death.

It was their judgment, however ill informed, that "it appears to us of the Jury that the child came to its death by violence."[87]

New Hampshire, like other colonies, had specific laws against infanticide. The 1759 "Act to Prevent the Murdering of Bastard Children" reads, in part,

Whereas many lewd women that have been delivered of bastard children, to avoid their shame, and to escape punishment do secretly bury or conceal the death of their children, and after, if the child be found dead, the said woman to allege that the said child was born dead. Whereas it falleth out sometimes, (altho' hardly it is to be proved) that the said child or children were murdered by the said women their lewd mothers, or by their assent or procurement:

Be it therefore Executed by the Governor, Council, and Representatives convened to General Assembly, and by the Authority of the same:

That if any woman be delivered of any issue of her body, male or female, which if it were born alive should by law be a bastard, and they endeavor privately, either by drowning, or secret burying thereof, that it may not come to light, whether it was born alive or not, but being concealed; in every such case the mother so offending shall suffer death, as in case of murder.[88]

According to the account in the *New Hampshire Gazette*, the subsequent trial

lasted from Ten O'Clock A.M. to Six in the afternoon. The following morning, the jury brought in their verdict, convicting Ruth Blay of "private burial and concealment of her Bastard child at South Hampton…contrary to our Peace, Crown, and Dignity and against the Law in such cases made and provided, and to the Evil example of others."[89]

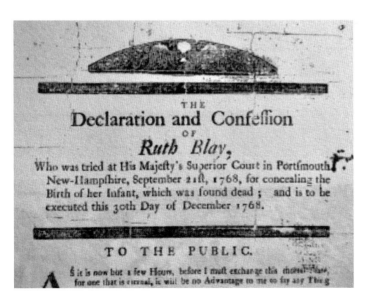

Ruth Blay's published confession. *Courtesy of Wikimedia Commons.*

The jury sentenced her "for the Burial and Concealement aforesaid, is condemned to suffer the pains of Death, in hanging by her neck, till her Body be dead."[90]

Ruth Blay was ordered to be hanged on November 4, 1768, but through reprieves from the original jury, magistrates and the governor, the actual hanging and the spectacle that was made of it did not occur until December 30.

Connecticut was the last to execute a female for the murder of a child, but in this particular case, while the victim was age six, the convicted murderer was but twelve years old.

Hannah Occuish lost both her parents, her Pequot mother and African American father, at a young age and was shuffled from one home to another in the town of New London until she was indentured at the age of twelve.

It was while indentured that she met six-year-old Eunice Boyles, and she may have been threatened by the younger girl's accusation of the theft of strawberries that Hannah had picked herself while walking. Whatever desperation she felt led her to commit murder when, on July 21, 1786, she lured the younger girl into the woods with the promise of a piece of calico before beating and strangling Eunice and then covering her body with large stones.

A neighbor walking in the woods soon discovered the cairn, and authorities quickly obtained a confession from Hannah. A swift trial was held in the meetinghouse, and after her conviction, a gallows was built behind the building, near the corner of what is now Granite Street.

Hannah's hanging was a public spectacle as well, with the Reverend Henry Channing from Yale College delivering a long sermon to an overflow crowd. The *Hartford Courant* printed a description of the execution and Hannah's composure on the gallows: "She seemed greatly afraid…but said little to anyone." Then "she thanked the Sheriff for his kindness, and launched into the eternal world."[91]

Capital punishment continued to be applied to a variety of crimes in New England courts well into the nineteenth century. As historian Alberton notes,

Twenty-one men and two women went to the gallows or faced the firing squad in Boston during the second half of the eighteenth century.… Besides being primarily male, Boston's executed were relatively young—on averaged aged twenty-six—and mostly poor. Their occupations placed them among the lower classes. There were 10 laborers, 5 mariners, 2 soldiers, a bricklayer and a slave.[92]

In Rhode Island, sixteen men were hanged between 1670 and 1845. There were twenty-six convicted pirates hanged on July 19, 1723, alone. The executed in both Providence, Newport and Kings County within those years includes eleven White men, three Black men and two Indigenous men.[93]

In the state where Quakers had long held power, it took a long reckoning after their loss of power to return to being a state of mercy when it came to capital crimes. That changed in the aftermath of the trial of John Gordon, the brother of a tavern owner who was charged with the murder of mill owner and Temperance leader Amasa Sprague.

Sprague was a progressive mill owner whose calico-dyeing mill was considered among the most modern and efficient at the time. Sprague was also among the active temperance activists as the movement to ban liquor grew in the early nineteenth century. He felt that Nicholas Gordon's nearby tavern was a distraction for his workers that hindered their punctuality and efficiency.

Gordon ran the tavern with his younger brothers John and William, who had recently arrived from Ireland. Sprague held a great deal of influence in public affairs at the time, and his motion to the state board of licenses resulted in the closing of Gordon's establishment.

When the forty-five-year-old entrepreneur left his Cranston, Rhode Island mansion after a hearty meal on New Year's Eve 1843, he was at the height of his wealth and influence. As he crossed the bridge over the river that gave his mill its needed power, he was assaulted by two men. A bullet fired into his right forearm disabled him from protecting himself from the savage beating that followed. His death was caused by blows from a blunt instrument to both sides of his skull.

When Sprague's beaten and bloodied body was found by his house servant, his gold watch and sixty dollars were still in his pocket. With robbery removed as a motive, suspicion soon fell on the Irish bar owner Gordon.

The era of large-scale production mills like Sprague's attracted unprecedented numbers of immigrants eager to work in America. During this time, the overwhelming majority were Irish Catholics, whose "popish worship" and culture of imbibing alcohol were seen as a moral threat by the Protestant elites running the city and state.

Gordon and Sprague had confronted each other publicly while the embattled tavern keeper faced losing his license, with Sprague allegedly grabbing Gorton by the collar and calling him a "damned Irishman."[94]

Others thought the killing might be politically motivated, as Sprague; his brother William, a state senator; and other cronies had recently put down the infamous Dorr Rebellion, a protest against longstanding voting laws that prohibited the majority of citizens from taking part in elections. Thomas Dorr, the leader of the rebellion, had been arrested but two months before. It was well known that Irish immigrants were among the strongest supporters of the rebellion. After Gordon was arrested and charged, those in his Irish community of Knightsville rallied to raise funds for his defense.

Gordon was convicted in a trial that had all the trappings of class prejudice. His two younger brothers and even his dog (who was suspected of biting Sprague's neck) were brought before the court. The brothers were found innocent of any involvement in the murder but charged with obstruction of justice. The dog was found to be "old and toothless," but the jury followed the judge's instructions to "give greater weight to Yankee witnesses" rather than the Irish witnesses brought before them by the defendant's counsel.

John Gordon was convicted and hanged on February 14, 1845. Thousands of Irish immigrants from throughout New England attended his funeral. The resultant outcry against the verdict and its blatant anti-immigrant and anti-Catholic message led to reforms within the state, including the banning of capital punishment. The death sentence has never been reinstated in the State of Rhode Island, and John Gordon was officially pardoned by Governor Lincoln D. Chafee on June 29, 2011.

CHAPTER 3

UNFORTUNATE ENDS

Early Inquiries into Causes of Death, Notifications, Early Obituaries

When death came in a community, a general inquiry, or investigation, was made to determine its cause. A body of men would be chosen, no matter their forensic experience or the circumstances or sex of the deceased. Most jurors were farmers rather than pharmacists. So in effect, jury duty, as we know it today, was a far more sobering assignment in early colonial towns.

To be called to be among those six or twelve men chosen to decipher the facts and consider the case that should go before the general court and its judges meant that an individual was summoned to investigate any violent assault, robbery or death within the community. Escorted by the sheriff and one or more assistants, the men were taken to the scene of the accident or crime. Evidence obtained by the investigation was viewed by the jury, as was the scene itself. Interviews with witnesses were conducted that day whenever possible, and one member of the group was chosen to record the testimonies and views of the twelve jurors about the case.

These inquiries were held especially important at times of death in the town or village. Letters and journals from the era of early settlements are filled with notations of the deaths of individuals, whether by natural means or, most often, by accidental occurrence.

Governor of Massachusetts Bay Colony John Winthrop's journals include a brief entry from October 1640 that reads: "Quere, of the child at Cambridge killed by a cat."[95] No later entry refers to the case.

Portrait of John Winthrop.
Published in Winthrop's
Journal, *Scribner & Sons,*
1908.

Other odd entries relate to the consequences of drink, waywardness and foolhardiness, especially in the young. "A young man, a tanner in Boston," Winthrop noted in June 1641, "going to wash himself in a creek, said, jestingly 'I will go and drown myself now', which fell out accordingly; for by the slipperiness of the earth, he was carried beyond his depth, and having no skill to swim, was drowned, though company was at hand, and one in the water with him."[96]

Winthrop seems to have looked on such deaths brought by folly or ignorance to be a kind of justice wrought by the hand of God. Those who died violating the Sabbath he seemed especially attentive to record with an ecclesiastical view:

> *Upon the Lord's Day at Concord two children were left at home alone, one lying in a cradle, the other having burned a cloth, and fearing his mother might see it, thrust it into a haystack by the door (the fire not being quite out) whereby the hay and house were burned and the child in the cradle before they came from meeting.*

Archibald Thompson, of Marblehead, carrying dung to his ground in a canoe upon the Lord's Day, in fair weather and still water, it sunk under him in the harbor near the shores and he was never seen after.[97]

Many of these entries of accidental deaths had much to do with the perilous conditions New Englanders found could come throughout the year, especially in winter.

Mr. Peter and Mr. Darton, with one of Acomenticus, went from Pascataquack with Mr. John Ward, who was to be entertained there by their minister; and though it be but six miles, yet they lost their way, and wandered two days and one night without food or fire, in the snow and wet.

The group eventually made their way to the seaside, close to their intended destination, but others, as Winthrop noted, were not so fortunate:

Not long before, a Godly maid of the church of Linne, going in a deep snow from Medford homeward, was lost, and some of her cloths found after among the rocks.[98]

One of the earliest inquiries in the town of Providence, Rhode Island, was into the death of the unfortunate Margaret Goodwin, whom jurors determined on March 4, 1657, was killed either by the "terribleness of the crack of thunder on the second of the third month or the cold, being she was naked." Goodwin had seen her property impounded by the city in the time of "her distraction" after the death of her husband six years before, and she remained impoverished the remainder of her days.[99]

Margaret Goodwin was among the most vulnerable of her community. There was little recourse or assistance for those who had grown too infirm to make a living. Providence, like other neighboring towns, assigned a protector, usually a neighbor, to look after destitute individuals. As did the man assigned to supply Margaret Goodwin with bedding and wood for the winter, some took advantage of the town.

Children were also among the most vulnerable, if not to disease then to accidents and murder.

One of the first such inquiries in Newport, Rhode Island, was held in 1661 and involved a young slave of Governor Benedict Arnold and the son of Mr. John Clark, another government official. The following year, when the court of trials was held in Newport, the results of the inquiries were discussed:

Upon accation of some debate in this Court Concerning the Death of a young negar servant to Mr. benedict Arnold now governor in the year 1661 soe Called and alsoe Concearning the Death of a son of Mr. Joseph Clarke now assistant in the year 1662 the Court declares themselves fully satisfied in the proceedings taken by the towne of Newport and the officers therof to the Enquiers after the Death of the parsons aforesd and that the proceedings aforesyd were fully available sufficiente and unquestionable as to the Clearing of all parsons from all maner of guilt Relating to the Death of the parsons aforesd.[100]

On August 15, 1679, a jury to serve as a "Coroners' Inquest" was summoned to the home of Ephraim and Hannah Pearce in Providence to investigate the death of their daughter, Elizabeth. Neighbor Mehitteble Sprauge testified that

upon ocation of being...at the house of Ephraim pearce, and goeing home from thence homeward a little before the setting of the sun, hearing a sudden nooyse, looked about, and Saw Hannah pearce y' wife of Ephraim Run doune the Hill to y' well and there pulled out Elizabeth.

The witness returned at once to the house where she found that Hannah

had layd her sayd Daughter on ye Bedd, where this deponant sayeth to ye best of her understanding she found sayd Elizabeth pearce ...aged about one yeare and a halfe to be Absolutly Dedd....Sayd mother of ye sayd Childe did use what meanes they could to preserve life; but it Could not be for ye Childe as aforesd was Dedd.

Hannah Pearce testified that Elizabeth had gone out of the house with her elder sister and she could hear the children talking outside, but about half an hour later, the elder sister returned without Elizabeth. Hannah "then asked the sayd Childe where is your sister, she Answered, shee is gone doune that way, (which way led to ye well, and pond)."[101]

Assistant John Whipple recorded that "wee find that Elizabeth Pearce the Daughter of Ephraim and Hanah his wife...exadentally fell into the well, and was overwhelmed in water, and by the providence of God drownded."[102]

Investigating childhood fatalities would become all too commonplace and certainly no less sobering than when a jury was sent to investigate the sudden death of the young son of Lieutenant James Olney and his wife, Halelujah, which they determined to be "a natural death."[103]

In another case, twelve men were sent to the scene of a sudden death on the farm of Josiah Owen in late December 1723, where Owen's son "was found dead this present day: the verdict of this jury is that said Josiah Owen was killed accidentally by meanes of Josiah Owen Senior his carte whele running over his head."[104]

The Toll of Early Epidemics

Among the causes of death in early New England, the most prevalent was disease, whether by individual illness or, more commonly, the affliction of a multitude of victims during one of the waves of epidemics and mysterious fevers that seasonally visited New England communities.

Such was the prevalence of fatalities that swept scythe-like through communities in times of these epidemics that it seemed little had been gained in physicians' ability to treat the waves of flux, smallpox, measles and fever that routinely landed on New England's shores. The fact that so much of the region relied on maritime commerce was one reason that new and challenging illnesses visited these seaside communities as well as recurring illnesses brought into the pubs and inns by sailors and soldiers passing through.

Boston's Cotton Mather suffered the loss of his wife, Elizabeth, their infant twins and a two-year-old daughter during an outbreak of measles in the town during the fall of 1713. He would lament in a sermon later that "the dying of a child is like the tearing off of a limb" from the body.[105]

Twelve major outbreaks of smallpox in Massachusetts during the one hundred years between 1620 and 1720 caused an average of one out of every ten deaths in the colony. In 1721, when an epidemic affected some six thousand Bostonians, Mather openly supported inoculation, and for the first time in New England, Dr. Zabdiel Boylston inoculated more than two hundred people.

Influenza, or what was often called "malignant pleurisy," was also a common visitor to communities, with major outbreaks occurring in 1647 and 1697–98.

A New England–wide epidemic of diphtheria, or what was known then as "throat distemper," tore through the region between 1735 and 1740. It

Detail of "View of Boston" showing Third Church and meetinghouse, William Burgis from
The New England Meeting Houses of the 17th Century, 1702. *Author's collection.*

began with a child coming down with cold-like symptoms in Kingston, New Hampshire, in the spring of 1735; the supposed "cold" worsened into a sore throat, loss of appetite and fever. The disease attacked the tissue in the throat, nose and lungs with devastating effect.

The disease soon spread to other towns in New Hampshire, then north to Kittery, Maine. In the coming months, the illness would visit communities in Connecticut and western Massachusetts. More than five thousand individuals died during the five-year scourge of illness, 75 percent of them children.[106]

Many in the rural, agricultural communities relied on home remedies that might be written down in one of the many "home medical" pamphlets that were produced or even the family Bible. Most were simply passed down through family experience. Many such areas also had a knowledgeable midwife, who might suggest some treatment or procure the herbs needed for a remedy herself.

The mid- to late-eighteenth-century diary of Congregationalist minister Ezra Stiles shows that death was a nearly daily occurrence at such times of an outbreak of illness.

In March 1772, Stiles recorded the rising tide of fatalities from an unknown illness. On the twenty-second of the month, he recorded "fifteen deaths in this town the week past, four times the common mortality here." The following day, he wrote again of this

> very sickly time, a universal Cold which becomes either Peri-pneumonia or Pleurisy as it seats in the Lungs or side. A very dying time. This day I visited thirty families, and come home at night greatly fatigued and sick myself.[107]

In October 1778, the Reverend Peleg Burroughs recorded the toll that another illness took in the last two weeks of the month alone on the communities of Tiverton and Little Compton, Rhode Island:

> 13. Early this morning I went down to the 4 corners on worldly business and to visit Elizabeth Corey and some others yet sick from the common and prevailing disorder of the bloody purging....Hearing that my neighbor Campbell the minister was sick with this disorder, I visited him this evening.

> 15. This day...I attended and preached at the funeral of Peleg Fish (a young lad 9 or 10 years old) son of John Fishs' widow. Then visited Amon Taber (at the point of death)...and in the evening visited and prayed with my neighbor Campbell, many other neighbors being present.

The gravestone of eight-year-old Elizabeth Peck, Palmer River Cemetery, Rehoboth, Massachusetts. *Photo by author.*

17ᵗʰ…Once more visited Amon Taber, from whence I proceeded to John Taber's with whom I had some peculiar talk and after I parted with him was obliged by the power of truth to return and say something more, taking leave of him in a most solemn manner.

Returned home and took my wife with me to visit the widow Sanford, and my old sick neighbor Campbell, who for some time (while I was there) seemed almost deprived of his reason, but a length revived so as to ask me to pray for him.…

21ˢᵗ. At eleven o'clock this forenoon I attended (as a neighbor) the funeral of Othniel Campbell (a Presbyterian minister, as he was called, aged 83) who died yesterday morning about 3 o'clock. His corps was carried to the Meeting House about noon, and finding many people together, I was enabled to say a few words, and pray with them.…

22ⁿᵈ…I spent the evening chiefly at Brother Samuel Taber's and just now closed it by reading and prayer at home, after which I fell into some very solemn and peculiar reflections about my neighbor Campbell and other neighbors lately deceased....

24th...Hearing that Sister Earl (Daniel's wife) was sick, I visited and prayed with her, accompaneyed by my wife....Visited the widow Rogers, old Samuel Snell, and John Weeden's wife at Elizabeth Davenport's where most all in the house were sick.

25th...Went down to the house of Joseph Brightman and preached again with Wonderful assistance (but from no particular text) at the funeral of Hannah Wilcox (aged about 20 years).

26. After doing some hard work and tending my forenoon school, I sat off (as soon as school was done) and went near 3 miles to the funeral of a daughter of Ephraim Mackomber's at the house of Benjamin Mackomber....

31st...Last 3rd day I was sent for to attend (on the 4th day) the funeral of a grandchild of Samuel Munyon's....Yesterday I was desired to visit a woman who was sick at the house of Joseph Gibbs.[108]

For ministers and physicians, these times were perhaps the most challenging to both their faith and physic. Many served for years only to die of illness themselves, a particularly cruel loss to many New England communities.

Even as science advanced to develop vaccines for identifiable diseases such as smallpox, communities ravaged by such diseases proved both fearful and skeptical of their effect and voted down inoculations in town for generations. The aforementioned Ezra Stiles took his family from Newport to New Haven to be inoculated during a later outbreak.

FATAL ACCIDENTS

Accidents of day-to-day life in early New England were also the cause of many deaths. Drownings occurred all too frequently in seaside communities, less so in rural places, where brooks and ponds were the dangers when both children and adults ventured on less-than-solid ice.

When unforeseen incidents or injuries caused death, it was often because of the lack of any type of antiseptic that could be applied to even the smallest wound. As late as 1798, Daniel Updike, the wealthy and well-educated heir of a Rhode Island plantation, had copied in his daybook "a cure for the bite of a mad dog," which was basically to rinse the wound with fresh water repeatedly, upward of twenty-five times after the wound was received.

Diarist Joshua Hempstead of New London, Connecticut, would write of the fate a family faced with even the smallest accident:

> *Wm Beebe had a Daughter died by a wound She Recd about 2 or 3 days ago In falling down with a knife in her Pocket wch Ran into her Belly yt her Caul came out 5 or 6 inches wch was cut off & the hole Sewed up but ye wound being deep proved mortal. She was 6 years old.* [109]

In 1728, Minister John Comer recorded a curious incident of accidental death in his diary that seemed to have been a premonition:

> *Friday, May 31, About 3 P.M., one Deborah Grinman (Greenman) was kill'd with thunder at Narragansett. There were some things remarkable in her death. Two nights before she dreamed yt a woman lay dead in ye same spot she was struck down in, She told her sister of it under great surprise, and yt she was kill'd with thunder. In ye morning of ye day in which she was kill'd twas very clear, but she apprehended it would be a fatal day. And when ye cloud arose she said* there is yt which will do ye business. *Accordingly, she was kill'sd in ye same spot. She was burned on ye side of her face, and her instep was broke. At ye time she had a child in her arms, which was stunned, but soon recovered.* [110]

Most common, of course, were those accidents of everyday life and work that occurred when men and women had to make ends meet and provide for their families in often less-than-safe conditions. A fall from a scaffolding, the collapse of a chimney, a wound from a tool—all were potentially fatal to a craftsman or mason. Sailors who had spent months at sea drowned in small port town harbors. Brewers and tanners alike fell into and perished in the massive vats that gave them their livelihood. Housewives would step too close to the fire and suddenly be engulfed in flames. Children were fatally scalded, fell down wells or, as we've seen, were crushed by carts or other farm equipment.

Leaving home could be just as treacherous. Travelers on horseback were sometimes thrown fatally off the road; horse-drawn carriages overturned when careening along unfamiliar roadways.

Leaving home for a lengthy ocean voyage was even more uncertain. Mariners, whether they were signed aboard fishing boats, whalers, merchant ships or military vessels, certainly faced the peril that New Englanders feared most: loss at sea.

So often was news relayed back to a home port of the loss of a ship with all hands that the literal and figurative picture of a spouse or engaged woman gazing earnestly at the horizon from the rocky shore became a symbol in poems, novels and paintings of the sacrifice made at home. Wealthy captains' wives watched the sea from aptly named "widow's walks," rail-enclosed platforms, usually surrounding small octagonal or tower-like structures above the rooflines of the elegant sea captains' homes that can still be found in New England's coastal towns.[111]

Such tragedy was also made most palpable when shipwrecks occurred in the waters off these same communities and the litter of cargo, rigging, sails and drowned bodies was thrown onto their own shorelines. In those communities with lighthouses, the keeper would raise the alarm when a foundering ship was sighted, and he (or she) with a group of volunteers would steer their own vessels to the site and save who they could from the waves.

In Massachusetts, the fifty-mile stretch of water along Cape Cod's coastline has long been known as an "ocean graveyard," which, with its constantly changing offshore shoals, has caused the demise of some three thousand vessels. These waters were especially treacherous during colonial times, when captains often had to rely more on experience than navigational charts and the rocky shoreline was often lit only with a faint beacon that was barely discernable in a raging storm. All the towns and villages along the coast shared these grim experiences. Plymouth County, Massachusetts, alone witnessed and assisted in rescues during seventeen shipwrecks between 1766 and 1805.

In the mid-nineteenth century, lifeguard rescue stations were formed, allowing whole teams of trained rescuers to be sent to the scene of a maritime disaster. Those men who served in what would later become the United States Coast Guard saved the lives of many crewmen in the region's maritime industry.

DEATH DUE TO MENTAL ILLNESS

Winters were especially feared in New England from its earliest settlement by Europeans. They were bleak and often despairingly cold. The streets and hovels of these small communities were often blanketed with snow and darkened by the soot that fell from the chimneys of surrounding houses. The winters were, as illustrated earlier, a time of shared sickness in communities, and often, especially in remote locations, the illnesses suffered were more than the fevers and yearly ailments that inhabitants had come to expect.

Depression and other forms of mental illness affected many, both women and men. Cases of suicide and extraordinary behavior were recorded in the journals of ministers and magistrates alike.

In 1637, Governor Winthrop recorded an unfortunate incident that occurred in Weymouth, Massachusetts:

> *February 6. A man of Weymouth (but not of the church) fell into some trouble of mind, and in the night cried out, "art thou come Lord Jesus?" and with that leapt out of his bed in his shirt, and, breaking from his wife, leaped out at a high window into the snow, and ran about seven miles off, and being traced in the snow, was found dead next morning. They might perceive, that he had kneeled down to prayer in divers places.*

A few years later, in the spring of 1642, his *Journal* records another tragic episode:

> *A cooper's wife of Hingham, having been long in a sad melancholic distemper near to phresy* [frenzy], *and having formerly attempted to drown her child, but prevented by God's gracious providence, did now again take an opportunity, being alone, to carry her child, aged three years, to a creek near her house, and stripping it of the clothes, threw it into the water and mud. But the tide being low, the little child scrambled out, and taking up its clothes, came to its mother who was set down not far off. She carried the child again, and threw it in so far as it could not get out; but then it pleased God, that a young man, coming that way, saved it. She would give no other reason for it, but that she did it to save it from misery.*[112]

In those early days of settlement, looking after those affected by mental illness was a shared responsibility. Those without adequate care at home relied on neighbors for assistance, and for those without family, early

Seventeenth-century-style window at the Eleazor Arnold House, 1693, Lincoln, Rhode Island. *Courtesy of Historic New England.*

efforts at poor relief brought them under an appointed guardian.

Before the advent of temperance committees in New England towns, many also dealt with the ravaging effects of alcoholism on families and, often, communities as a whole. One tragic example is the case of Jeremiah Meacham.

Meacham was born in Salem, Massachusetts, but grew up mainly in the Boston area. As an adult, he removed to Newport, Rhode Island, married and raised two children there. Once in Rhode Island, however, Meachum abandoned the constraints of his rigid upbringing and "fell in with some who were openly wicked in Providence." He stopped attending church and openly criticized Christianity.[113]

As this was Rhode Island, no punishment was issued for Meacham's missed attendance at Sabbath, and in other respects, he continued to be a model citizen. However, he continued to grow disenchanted with his life and fell to consuming large quantities of hard liquor.

On March 21, 1715, Meacham was observed walking around town in great distress. The following morning, he was observed on the roof of his house, fearful, it seemed, even of those who passed on the street below. He shouted at passersby that he meant to hurt no one and wished only to be left alone. When his wife and sister made the fateful decision to convince him to come back into the house and receive comfort, he turned on them, stabbing his wife with a penknife and dispatching both women with an axe.[114]

As in earlier times, the social responsibility of tending to the troubled souls of even the most hardened criminals fell to the clergy of the town. They visited prisons and hospitals, tended to their own congregation and were often those who recorded the tragic episodes that occurred in their towns, including attempted suicides.

NEIGHBORS WITH SOME FORM of mental illness were not uncommon, but as might be expected, the rate of suicide was greater in the rural towns of New England than those more heavily populated and often came in a violent manner.

Twenty-one-year-old Reverend John Comer of Swansea, Massachusetts, and later Newport, Rhode Island, recorded several incidents one summer of individuals attempting to end their lives.

In August 1726, he recorded,

> *This month a hardened young man being committed to prison for theft, attempted to kill himself by stabbing an Awl into his bowels, and to choke himself by tying his stockings straight about his neck, but was prevented. I being sent for of about 9 o'clock at night to pray for him he appeared ye most awful spectacle yt I ever beheld, for I plainly discovered ye sad symptoms of a hard and obdurate heart.*[115]

In September, Comer wrote in his diary,

> *About ye middle of this month one Hannah Suderick, a disconsolate young woman as is supposed, drowned herself about 11 of ye clock at night. The*

Stone well in Putnam, Connecticut. *Photo by author.*

74

town was alarmed by ye beat of ye drum (the ground why isn't certainly known) And in ye afternoon of ye next day one Catherine Cook attempted ye like action, but was discovered after she had fallen into ye water; but upon examination…she seemed to be under ye power of Satan in a very awful manner.[116]

The following year in early winter, the Reverend Comer noted,

This morning about break of day, a stranger newly from England who kept at Mr. Thomas Richardson's (who had been observed to labour melancholy) got out of bed and went down in his shirt and threw himself into the well, and was there found drowned.

Vermont farmer Hiram Harwood expressed shock and dismay at the suicides in his native town of Bennington. Learning that his neighbor Gustav Walbridge had hanged himself in his father's attic, Harwood could only conclude that "he committed this awful deed in a fit of insanity." Another neighbor, Saxton Pickett, "in a fit of despair, which grew out of a course of intemperance that he had been *in* a few years past…cut his throat with a razor from ear to ear & died instantly." Another man, Smith Crawford, who was Harwood's own age, also slit his throat "in a most shocking manner."[117]

THE FIRST OBITUARIES

Formal notices of death were, in early years, placed on meetinghouse or tavern doors, though word of mouth still reigned as the primary form of communication in many villages throughout the eighteenth century. If the deceased was a prominent member of the town or village, a broadside might be printed to commemorate his funeral and include the praises neighbors scripted onto slips of paper and left on the bier when paying their respects.

For most, however, any written notice of death occurred formally in the notes of the inquest, if one was held, or in the inventory, or property evaluation, of the deceased. Notations appeared less formally in the handwritten pages of the family Bible or the diary of a relative or neighbor. The advent of the colonial press and its popularity would provide the first printed notices of death for the communities at large. These were often sparse in early newspapers, unless extenuating and newsworthy circumstances surrounded the death.

Among the first newspapers in colonial New England was the *Boston News-Letter*, which made its appearance in 1704 and was so successful that it did not face competition until the founding of the *Boston Gazette* in 1719. Neighboring Rhode Island brought out its own *Rhode Island Gazette* in 1732, but it lasted less than a year. The *American Newport Mercury* was established around the same time and had evolved into the *Newport Mercury* by 1758; it remained that city's longstanding newspaper. The *Providence Gazette and Country Journal* would follow in 1762 and become among the preeminent newspapers in New England during the colonial period.

The Green family of Connecticut published the first newspapers in that colony, beginning with Timothy Green and the establishment of the *New London Summary* in 1758 and his nephew Thomas Green, who founded Hartford's *Connecticut Courant* a decade later. Thomas Green had also taken over the *Connecticut Gazette* of New Haven by 1760. He and his brother Samuel would convert this newspaper into the *Connecticut Journal* in 1767.

In 1773, the *Norwich Packet* emerged. It was begun by publishers Alexander and James Robertson, along with John Trumbull; the Loyalist brothers had gone to New York by 1776, leaving Trumbull the sole owner. Under his direction, the paper flourished, and his son would continue to publish the paper as the *Connecticut Centinel* in the early nineteenth century.

While much national news was reprinted from other newspapers,

> *town news was contributed by citizens or perhaps by the printer himself. Aside from politics and law, articles could be about anything current in the community, from the mundane to the sensational, the latter including reports of whirlwinds, tornadoes, floods, murders, seductions and theft. Local people who wished to remain anonymous sometimes submitted articles or poems, signing them with pen-names, such as "Censor," "Plato," and "Friend of Liberty."*[118]

Local news included the first obituaries published in New England newspapers, which were but brief mentions, like these gleaned from editions of the *Newport Mercury* from 1774 to 1799:

> *April 25, 1774, Stanton, Benjamin, last Tuesday, found in a gully near Baker's Spring with his head cut.*

Front page of the *Norwich Packet*. *Courtesy of Wikimedia Commons.*

May 30, 1774, Smith, Mrs. Sarah, last Thursday, her son Isaac was married about the same time.

January 2, 1775, Morgan, Mrs. Elizabeth, a noted mid-wife.

June 12, 1775, Hudson, John, carpenter, fell from stage.

October 2, 1775, Bristow, William, son of Widow ___ Bristow, drowned from capsizing a boat, aged 23 years.

July 13, 1782, Hookey, Betsey, drowned ___ Lydia, drowned.

May 15, 1786, Irish, Constant, of Charles, aged 20 years, drowned from a scow this morning at Newport.
___, Jonathan, of Charles, aged 25 years, drowned from a scow this morning at Newport.

July 14, 1795, Allen, Paschel, at Hopkington, said to be 116 years old.

October 20, 1795, Aldrich, Thomas, died at Meeting in East Greenwich, very aged.

August 26, 1797, Gibbs, John, of George, (brother of Governor William C.) accidentally shot.

May 14, 1799, Clarke, Samuel Ward, of Ethan, of Newport, aged 20 years, on board ship Semiramis…a day before arrival in Canton.

August 10, 1799, Congdon, John, son of John (Esq.) killed by lightening at Prudence Isle.[119]

When the first issue of the *Providence Gazette and Country Journal* rolled off the press, the slogan beneath its banner read, "Containing the Freshest of Advices both Foreign and Domestic." This was true of the obituaries published as well, informing the reader of the demise of political, social

Front page of the *Providence Gazette. Courtesy of Wikimedia Commons.*

and eccentric individuals from around the world as well as the nation. The *Gazette* also published notices of local deaths in a matter-of-fact manner similar to the *Mercury*.

December 30, 1762
Bosworth, ____ a negroe servant of Edward Bosworth, at Warren, fell backwards over a stone Near his master's door, fractured his skull so severely that he died in a few minutes.

January 29, 1763
Carpenter, Colonel ____, of Rehobeth, thrown from his horse on journey between Providence and Boston.

February 11, 1763
Bennet, ____. At Coventry, killed by the falling of a tree.

April 4, 1764
Brown, Allen, Esq.; his two negroe servants were sailing a deeply laden scow down the river, the scow sank about two miles from shore and one was drowned.

March 15, 1765
Aborn, ____, eldest son of Captain Samuel, aged 9 years, fell into the stream of the bolting mill and drowned.

July 30, 1767
Brown, ____, son of Nicholas, age 4 years, fell from a wharf and drowned.

July 13, 1769
Brown, Lemuel of Natic, Mass. Drowned from Nathan Dagget's wooden boat above the upper ferry on Pawtucket River.

June 5, 1773
Clarke, Elisha, drowned while washing sheep at South Kingstown.

June 12, 1773
Beadle, Christopher; a deranged man, jumped from a vessel near Starvegoat Island, by help of a spar drifted to a rock a mile eastward, where he remained till morning, from where it is supposed he drowned, June 3, 1773; June 9, the body was found near Sabin's Point and interred.

February 25, 1775
Barton, Andrew, of Pawtuxet, his child fell into a kettle of boiling water,
died three days after.

September 12, 1776
Arnold, Rufus, at Smithfield, killed by the recoil of his gun.

February 25, 1778
Barnes, Levi
Barnes, Peleg, drowned in crossing the river from Warwick in a boat.

October 21, 1780
Briggs, Joseph of Scituate, after attempting to murder his wife.

Such scarcity of information was rarely embellished, most often in a case of a remarkable or extraordinary death, as in the case of Mrs. Martha Burr:

Wife of Elisha, and daughter of Col. Peleg Gardiner of Swansea. She
was married to Mr. Burr February 7, 1795; was subject to insane freaks.
On one occasion swallowed a silver spoon which was taken from her
stomach after death, a period of 185 weeks after being swallowed....She
finally caused her death by tying a string around her throat which caused
strangulation. At Rehoboth.

On June 1, 1822, a notice was printed of the strange passing of nineteen-year-old William Bosworth of Denneysville, Maine, who "with others went out to shoot an eagle, being fatigued, he sat down and instantly expired, complained of a pain in his side."

The *Providence Journal* made its first appearance on January 3, 1820, as a semiweekly paper, published on Mondays and Thursdays. The gleanings that follow are taken from the first decade of the newspaper's existence and reflect the advent of "death journalism," with often graphic descriptions of the subject's death, feeding the public's continued fascination with the unfortunate ends of ordinary and extraordinary people from the region and around the world.

March 30, 1821
Taylor, Charles, aged 18 years, while standing on Weybosset Bridge he fell
(probably in a fit) into the water and was drowned.

November 26, 1821
Bond, Sarah, in England, a very eccentric character, a miser and recluse, having a bitter dislike of men whom she called "beasts" and women something worse, declared she had no blood relative on earth, had, in 1812, L45,000 in funds who she said only the King could have.

December 20, 1821
Treadwell, Bradley, at Weston, CT., aged 31 years, was supposed dead; revived after 4 hours; said he had seen a beautiful city and then died.

March 23, 1822
Sumner, Keriah, wife of Ebenezer, aged 59 years at Milfred, Mass., after an illness of 4 years. She had drawn from her 2041 pounds of water, allowing a pint to weigh a pound and 32 gallons to a barrel, she had eight barrels, lacking one pint.

January 20, 1823
Gardiner, George, at Newburyport in a scuffle with Thomas Langdon, who in falling, struck his eye against a cane, which pierced the brain, killing him instantly.

June 27, 1827
Carr, Miss Betsey Miller, of Capt. Caleb, 2nd, in 21st year, at Warren, she was returning home from a visit to a neighbor with friends and was so frightened at some real or imaginary object by the wayside, as to cause her immediate death.

February 6, 1828
Woodruff, James, at Fayette, N.Y., aged 47 years; he said an angel told him in a dream to keep beastly drunk for 9 days and nights, and if he survived he would be saved; he drank a gallon a day and would be saved but did not survive.

Such obituaries grew as newspapers and their readership continued to expand throughout the region. Often, in order to increase readership, accounts of unusual or sensational deaths from around the country, even the world, were printed and reprinted in New England newspapers.

CHAPTER 4

UNSOUND ENDINGS

Strange Disappearances, Ghostly Sightings, Tales Both Tall and True

Some years ago, during my journey through the voluminous shelves of books written on New England history, I came upon an incredible story that seemed tailor-made for an exploration of such accounts— or tall tales—that filled the pages of America's early newspapers.

The story first appeared in the *New England Magazine* in 1824 under the authorship of one Jonathan Dunwell, who, much in the style of newspaper reporting at the time, retold the haunting tale of "Peter Rugg: The Missing Man." When the story was reprinted in the *New England Galaxy* shortly after, many readers interpreted the telling as a true story.

Rugg was a wealthy cattle and horse merchant who gave his family a fine home on Middle Street in Boston, Massachusetts. He often took short business excursions in a light carriage drawn by his favorite horse, a great, black, Roman-nosed bay. Horse and carriage became a fixture on the street as Rugg departed and arrived home from these day trips.

Such was the case in the summer of 1770 when he planned a short visit to the town of Concord and back, to be accomplished in a single day, even if his carriage arrived after nightfall. At the last minute, Rugg agreed to let his ten-year-old daughter, Jenny, accompany him. They left early the next morning in fine weather and reached Concord without delay. On their return, however, the pair and their horse and carriage were overtaken by a furious thunderstorm. They were fortunate to have an acquaintance nearby named Tom Cutter, who welcomed them into his West Cambridge home.

Drawing of Peter Rugg and daughter. *From Samuel Drake's* New England Legends and Folklore.

Cutter reportedly led Rugg's daughter to warm herself by the fire while he served a dram of warm spiced rum to his visitor.

Despite Cutter's offer to let the pair wait out the storm, Rugg insisted on leaving and drove his carriage back out into the tempest, determined to reach home by nightfall. The chaise never arrived home. In the coming months, authorities searched for any clues whatsoever of the disappearance, and the family offered a large reward, hoping for answers, but no trace of the father and daughter was found.

Just after midnight one morning the following spring, the occupants of the houses along Middle Street were awakened by the sound of hooves on the cobblestone roadway. Peering out his window, neighbor Thomas Felt recognized the unmistakable chaise of Peter Rugg and his great bay trotting down the street, enclosed, as he told it, within a kind of phosphorescent glow. Within days, similar tales of a ghostly carriage were reported throughout the region.

Enthusiastic readers wrote to the *Galaxy* asking for more details of the story, and subsequent serial publications popularized the tale and led to a string of accounts by witnesses that had seen the apparition.

Postman Andanoah Adams claimed to have been overtaken by the carriage while delivering mail in Newburyport. The chaise spooked his horses, causing them to pull his wagon off the road. He, too, witnessed a glowing carriage and swore that he saw the apparitions of Rugg and his frightened daughter at her father's side as he gripped the reins.

The author also claimed to have witnessed the apparition while on a business trip from Boston to Providence. The coach being full, he sat up front with the driver and so witnessed the ghostly chaise driving past at an unearthly speed. The driver told Dunwell that he had seen the apparition many times and that the driver sometimes stopped and asked the route to Boston. Such sightings, the driver informed the author, often preceded a great thunderstorm.

Seemingly the most credible witness to appear in the story was the Reverend Samuel Nickels, who claimed to have encountered the apparition while riding on the Post Road from the village of Wickford, Rhode Island, to the town of Providence. Shortly after leaving Wickford on an old mare, Nickels found himself in a driving rainstorm as the horse plodded through Quonset. As the road carried them through a narrow divide between a great hill and a rock ledge, the minister, huddled in the saddle, looked up at the sound of oncoming hoofbeats and witnessed the chaise coming straight at

Devil's Foot Ledge, North Kingstown, Rhode Island. *Photo by author.*

him. He could clearly see the man frantically pulling on the reins and the frightened girl gripping his arm beside him.

The minister's horse threw him briefly onto the back of the passing bay before it bolted with the chaise onto the ledge, where its hoofmarks can still be viewed today.

A poignant addition to the tale was that, years later, a man and a small girl, soaked by rain although it had been a clear day, knocked at the door of their old address, puzzled about why the door and the general appearance of the house had changed. The child recognized the large footstone (front step) on which she had sat and eaten her bread and drunk milk, but all else had seemingly changed.

As the years passed, the story was reprinted, most notably in Samuel Adams Drake's popular *New England Legends and Folklore* in 1883, which has been reprinted many times. In more recent times, popular local histories have retold the tale of the ghostly chaise reappearing at numerous places throughout the region, often with the implication that it is a true story, while the truth itself has been lost to readers over the years.

The tale was originally written in the form of a letter and intended to be the passing of a yarn, a kind of New England tale on par with Irving's headless horseman of the same period. The author of the letter, attorney and part-time author William Austin, used the pseudonym Jonathan Dunwell. The style of the letter, including the use of a multitude of supposed witnesses, helped to create the illusion that it was a true story, even to the point of its modern inclusion in an encyclopedia of unexplained paranormal phenomena.

A story involving another well-to-do New England family and its mansion had its origins in a story that appeared in the *Nashua Gazette*.

The Tyng family's history in New England dates to 1639, when Edward Tyng purchased five hundred acres and named the tract Dunstable for his hometown in the United Kingdom. As the region flourished, it expanded to include the towns of Tyngsboro and Nashua. By the time of Edward's grandson Eleazer's marriage to Sarah Alford, the property held a spacious and luxuriously furnished mansion. A large, gambrel-roofed house with a four-columned porch as part of the front façade, it boasted a pair of great chimneys that made the mansion on the hill even more imposing.

Among the five children of Eleazer and Sarah who were raised in such privilege was Jonathan Tyng, who as a young man, was, by all appearances, the epitome of a well-heeled heir to an upper-crust fortune, attending a fine college and becoming engaged to a woman from a wealthy Boston family.

The Tyng Estate, Tyngsboro, Massachusetts. *Courtesy of the National Archives.*

Around the time of his engagement, however, he was introduced to Judith Thompson, who had the reputation of being one of the most beautiful women in New England. Doubtless she had many suitors, and perhaps driven by pride and jealousy, Tyng fell madly in love pursuing her.

While maintaining his lifestyle at the mansion house, he arranged to have a dubious acquaintance named Dr. Blood pose as a minister and perform a "wedding" for the benefit of the hapless girl and settled her immediately into a home in Nashua.

Tyng led this double life for some years, and the couple had two children together. When Judith became pregnant a third time, however, something changed in the relationship that brought it to a fatal and tragic end. Marriage to his wealthy bride-to-be was forthcoming, and Tyng was remodeling the family home. Seeking, no doubt, to prevent the exposure of his deceit to his fiancée and her family, he again sought the assistance of Dr. Blood in murdering his wife and children.

When the deed was done, the bodies were hidden under the new hearth being constructed at his mansion house. Jonathan Tyng is said to have kept his criminal act secret throughout his life. In 1771, as he lay on his deathbed, friends complained of being barred from seeing him until a lifelong friend forced his way into the mansion and his friend's bedroom, where he witnessed the ghost of Tyng's murdered wife appear and curse him, telling him his name would be forgotten, even erased from the fine stone that would lie engraved on his crypt.

The story continues that for many years after the brick foundation and heavy table-stone memorial were erected in the Tyngsboro Cemetery, the inscribed stone and later replacements came to have their inscriptions and epitaphs repeatedly wiped clean, as though by an unseen hand.

The mansion, meanwhile, was inherited by Tyng's sister Sarah, who occupied the house for the remainder of her life. Having never married and borne children, toward the end of her life, she was desperate to keep the house in the family, and she left the property to a nephew with the stipulation that he take the family name with the inheritance. For unknown reasons, he declined, and on Sarah's death, the mansion was abandoned and fell into disrepair.

All of this, however, was merely the backdrop for the fantastic tale reported in the *Nashua Gazette*.

Years after the death of Sarah Tyng and the abandonment of the mansion, a traveler happened on the house, his driver and carriage being hopelessly engulfed in a snowstorm until attracted by the lights of a large and beautiful house.

They stopped and knocked on the door, hoping to have a brief respite from the storm. They were greeted by an elegant woman dressed in a resplendent emerald gown, who welcomed the travelers inside. The house was the most luxurious either man had ever seen. After a hearty meal, the driver was given accommodations in a cozy apartment above the stables and the passenger shown to an elegantly furnished bedroom, where he soon retired.

With the coming of daylight, both men awoke in a decidedly different house than the one that had welcomed them the night before. Dust covered the windows and floors, what furniture remained was threadbare and broken and the heavy curtains that draped the shuttered windows hung in tatters to the floor.

The men left the house as quickly as they could and, when they made it into the neighboring town, sought out the local newspaper to tell their story. Locals quickly identified the beautiful host in the story as Judith Thompson, though no mention of children being seen or heard was ever made.

Tyng's grave remains in Drake Cemetery in Tyngsboro, Massachusetts, but the mansion house is gone. While it received recognition as a nationally registered landmark in 1977, it burned down just four years later, but not before stories of the appearance of Judith Thompson's ghost became so numerous that the legend became associated with the mansion house and

John York house, 1766. *Photo by author.*

the nearby cemetery. The tale is still printed in books and online blogs as a true story today.

Similar tales with some variations may be found elsewhere in New England, including Narragansett, Rhode Island. They seem to be of the "cautionary tale" genre, warning against the evils wrought by greed and coveting.

Taverns as well as mansions are also often the sites of such reputed hauntings. One such tavern house is the John York house of Stonington, Connecticut. Built in 1741 by John York, the house had become a tavern by the time of the Revolutionary War, situated—as it still remains—at the merging of two highways in southeastern Connecticut. The legend as it has been passed down concerns two local militiamen who shared drinks at the tavern one fateful night.

As the men drank and their conversation turned to the local women they had encountered, it soon became apparent that the woman whose affections both of them most desired to gain was one and the same. No doubt as the drinks increased and the night aged, the mood grew darker. At the end of the night, a fight broke out between them, and out of desperation for his own life, or in fury, one soldier drew a knife and plunged it into the other. So remorseful was the murderer for his act that he fled the scene and committed suicide that same night.

In the tavern, the Yorks could not remove the victim's blood from the floorboards. They removed the boards, turned them over and placed them back on the floor. As the legend recounts, from that time, unexplained noises, cold spots in the rooms and shadowy forms appeared throughout the house.

It's unclear when the house left the hands of the York family—both John York Jr. and his son John York III lived in Stonington their entire lives— but it was purchased in 1963 by Hugo and Miriam Wilms. They moved in with their family, which included three sons. When Miriam Wilms noticed the paranormal activity in the house, she conducted seances, which only increased the activity but offered no explanation of the source of the spirit's restlessness.

When one of their sons claimed to be attacked, the Wilms called in spiritualists Ed and Lorraine Warren, who, in their sessions within the house, identified the spirit as a Revolutionary War soldier. Their efforts to free the spirit from the house were believed to have been successful. After the Wilms moved out in 1987, the house was vacant for a decade.

The former York house was purchased, restored and turned into a bed and breakfast. While the new owners reportedly heard an odd voice now and again, and guests reported something unusual on occasion, paranormal activity at the site seemed to have quieted down, though the new owners themselves used the legend to promote sleepovers, especially around Halloween.

The present owner is also mindful of the legend and, working with local author Thomas D'Agastino and his wife, allowed a paranormal investigation within the house that provided an intriguing example of an electronic voice phenomenon (EVP). The author asked whether the murdered soldier was in the house, and the recording reveals an exasperated voice telling him to "get out," the words uttered with all the weariness the punishment for a tragically impulsive act nearly 250 years before can muster.

If such stories and even tall tales were believed by individuals in the nineteenth century, it was because there were more than enough actual occurrences of the unexplained in their lifetimes, as well as stories passed down through generations, to bolster the believability of a ghostly chaise on an eternal journey or ghosts inhabiting the houses in which they once lived or even visiting neighbors' houses. In those rural and provincial areas of America especially, these beliefs had a longevity well into the time that scientific and Enlightenment thought began to impact the cities and smaller capitals of the country.

Such occurrences of what is now called paranormal activity were often recounted in early journals. One of the more bizarre was written as an actual event in 1639 in what is now Brookline, Massachusetts.

In this year one James Everell, a sober, discreet man, and two others, saw a great light in the night at Muddy River. When it stood still, it flamed up, and was about three yards square; when it ran, it was contracted into the figure of a swine; it ran as swift as an arrow towards Charlton, and so up and down about two or three hours. They were come down to their lighter about a mile, and, when it was over, they found themselves quite back against the tide to the place they came from. Divers other credible persons saw the same light, after, about the same place.[120]

Later phenomena were widely circulated in newspapers, but often, one could find stories in local papers, as did Swedish minister Peter Kalm, who was traveling through North America, including various visits to New England.

On one of his journeys, Kalm copied down the notice of "A Curious Phenomenon" printed in the *American Weekly Mercury* of Newport, Rhode Island, on March 30, 1722, which read:

There has lately a surprising appearance been seen at Narragansett, which is the occasion of much discourse here, and is variously represented; but for the substance of it, it is a matter of fact beyond dispute, it having been seen by an abundance of people, and one night about 20 persons at the same time, who came together for that purpose. The truth, as near as we can gather from the relations of several persons, is as follows. This last winter there was a woman died at Narragansett of the small pox, and since she was buried, there has appeared, upon her grave chiefly, and in various other places, a bright light as the appearance of fire. This appearance commonly begins about 9 or 10 o'clock at night, and sometimes as soon as it was dark. It appears variously as to time, shape, place, and magnitude, but commonly in one entire body. The first appearance [is] commonly small, but increases to a great bigness and brightness, so that in a dark night they can see the grass and bark of the trees very plainly; and when it is at the height, they can see sparks fly from the appearance like sparks of fire, and the likeness of a person in the midst wrapt in a sheet with its arms folded.

This appearance moves with incredible swiftness, sometimes the distance of half a mile from one place to another in the twinkling of an eye. It commonly appears every night, and continues till break of day. A woman in that neighborhood says she has seen it every night for these six weeks past.[121]

Those who knew the stories of the tavern and the Tyng family ghosts would also likely have been familiar with the ghostly sightings that occurred over several years in the town of Sullivan, Maine.[122]

The incidents began in August 1799 in the home of Abel Blaisdel. One night, when sitting down to dinner, the family noticed a persistent knocking coming from the basement below. Blaisdel investigated but found nothing that would indicate why the knocking occurred. Despite repeated searches, the knocking continued through the fall and into winter, driving the family to the point of desperation.

At his wits' end, Blaisdel went into the cellar and demanded that the devil or whatever was the source tell him what it wanted. The reply sent him running up the stairs in fright and disbelief, for in calling forth the source of the knocking, he was addressed by the spirit of Nelly Butler, the deceased daughter of his neighbor Edward Hooper.

As Eleanor "Nelly" Hooper, she had married Captain George Butler, and the newlyweds found very soon that they were expecting their first child. As happened to many women at that time, the physical demands of giving birth brought tragic complications, and both Nelly and her infant died on

Early New England farmhouse. *Photo by author.*

the birthing bed on June 13, 1799. The pair were interred in an unmarked grave at nearby Butler's Point.[123]

Abner Blaisdel rode immediately to Hooper's house, just a few miles away, and told him of what had occurred. Hooper, naturally, was skeptical but was eventually persuaded to come to Blaisdel's house and attempt to make contact with the spirit of his daughter. Hooper would later record that "she gave such clear and irresistible tokens of her being the spirit of my own daughter as gave me no less satisfaction than admiration and delight."[124]

That summer, the spirit of Nelly Butler became increasingly active, appearing before Blaisdel's son Paul as he walked through the fields and following him as he fled in fear. She appeared outside the Blaisdel house numerous times and continued her visitations in the cellar of the home. As word carried of the haunting, the curious flocked to the town, and Blaisdel allowed some of the throng to camp on the property. One visitor recorded a group's experience of witnessing the apparition in the basement:

> At first the apparition was a mere mass of light, then grew into personal form, almost as tall as myself. We stood in two ranks about four or five feet apart. Between these ranks she slowly passed and re-passed, so that any of us could have handled her. When she passed by me, her nearness was that of contact: so that if there had been a substance, I should have certainly felt it....The glow of the apparition had a constant, tremulous motion.[125]

The Reverend Abraham Cummings was, as might be expected, the most skeptical of the neighbors, and he called on the Blaisdel house, alarmed by the effect such sightings were having on his congregation. He was determined to dispel the notion of any ghost in the household. Nonetheless, the spirit appeared to him as he rode through the nearby fields, "surrounded by a bright light."[126] He recognized the form inside the light as that of the deceased Nelly Butler.

The spirit soon informed Abner Blaisdel of the reason for her appearance: her widowed husband was courting Blaisdell's fifteen-year-old daughter. The captain being nearly twice her age, Blaisdell was reluctant to consent to the wedding, but the spirit of Nelly Butler told him that it was her "divine mission"[127] to see her husband remarried to his daughter. Captain Butler was also summoned to the house, where Nelly appeared to her husband in a winding sheet, holding her child. According to the later written account by the Reverend Cummings, when Butler tried to embrace his wife, his arms went right through her form. She appeared three times that day, imploring

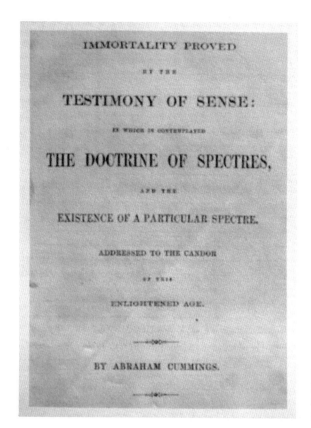

IMMORTALITY PROVED

BY THE

TESTIMONY OF SENSE:

IN WHICH IS CONTEMPLATED

THE DOCTRINE OF SPECTRES,

AND THE

EXISTENCE OF A PARTICULAR SPECTRE.

ADDRESSED TO THE CANDOR

OF THIS

ENLIGHTENED AGE.

BY ABRAHAM CUMMINGS.

Frontpiece of Reverend Cummings's *Doctrine of Spectres. Courtesy of Wikimedia Commons.*

him to remarry. Abner Blaisdel gave his blessing, and his daughter Lydia and George Butler were wed on May 29, 1800.

For nine days after the wedding, the visitations ceased, but on the tenth day, the spirit of Nelly Butler appeared before the newlywed couple to tell them that they would soon find that Lydia was with child but then tempered that joyful news by declaring that, as it had with her, the ordeal would bring the death of his young bride and their offspring.

The ghostly sightings then ceased for a little more than two months before the spirit became active once again, being witnessed by over one hundred people during the month of August, as she had been the year before.

The following March, 1801, Lydia Butler and her newborn died in childbirth, as the spirit had predicted. The pair were also buried on Butler's Point, near the grave of Nelly and her child. The spirit appeared once more to a large crowd gathered by the Reverend Cummings in 1806, who had by then become convinced that the spirit of Nelly was a messenger from heaven who could foretell the future. Cummings would author an account of the entire affair in his book *Immortality Proved by the Testimony of Sense: In Which Is Considered the Doctrine of Spectres, and the Existence of a Particular Spectre*, published in 1826.

While the minister may have been certain that the apparition had appeared from the hand of God, his flock and others in the county were not so certain that the devil himself did not have a hand in the visitations from what they now viewed as a malevolent spirit. They believed Lydia Butler's death and that of her child came about from a curse, not a foretold coincidence.

Today, Nelly Butler is considered the first recorded haunting in New England—that is, the first to be published in a book as well as the newer media of newspaper publishing.

Indeed, as incidents of paranormal activity occurred in later years, it seems such stories of tortured spirits or those bent on revenge became fodder for newspapers eager to expand their readership. Such newspapers and thence the stories would be widely read across the region and other parts of the nation as well.

CHAPTER 5

RITUALS OF REMEMBRANCE

Funeral Rites, Tokens and Memorials, the Burial Place

N ews of a death in early New England towns brought the neighbors to the house within hours. Women came to help wash and prepare the body for viewing as well as do the housework and prepare for the funeral feast. Men brought food and supplies and often, in small villages, built the coffin on-site for the body to be laid within. The time between death and burial of the body was relatively short, usually a day or two.

A feast was held the night before the funeral, and large quantities of rum, punch, wine and whiskey were often consumed. A perusal of the expenses related to the accidental drowning of one David Porter of Hartford in 1678 reveals that liquor was distributed to all involved with the tragedy:

—By a pint of liquor for those who dived for him..............*1 shilling*
—By a quart of liquor for those who brought him home........*2 shillings*
—By two quarts of wine and gallon of cyder to jury of inquest

At the funeral feast itself, eight gallons and three quarts of wine were consumed, at a cost of one pound, fifteen shillings. By comparison, the coffin in which Mr. Porter was laid to rest cost but twelve shillings.[128]

In preparation for the viewing, local custom—as in Hartford and surrounding towns in Connecticut—decreed that any mirrors, pictures or ornamentation in the home be draped with black cloth, and at times, the front shutters of a home would be closed and tied with black ribbon for the period of mourning, which could last up to a year.

If the deceased had lived in the village, the meetinghouse usually held the bier, or long table on which the coffin could be placed with candles, and a pall-cloth to be draped over the coffin, which was usually made of heavy black or purple fabric, sometimes velvet. This came to be a longstanding tradition. After the death of his aunt in the winter of 1711, farmer and carpenter Joshua Hempstead "went in ye morn to fetch ye black cloth thence to help carry out ye coffin and so to my Aunt's funeral."[129]

At the viewing, the early New Englanders carried over the Old Country tradition of writing laudatory verses or epitaphs that would be placed on the bier. In later years, these would often be collected and printed in colonial broadsides, often embellished with death's-heads, skulls and crossbones, caskets, scythes and hourglasses, symbols of death all too familiar to New Englanders.

Early burials in New England were simple and somber affairs. Prayers and eulogies were eschewed over the grave as popish, or Catholic, practices. Instead, as Thomas Lecheford noted in his early *Plain Dealing, or Newes from New England*:

> *At Burials nothing is read, nor any funeral sermon made, but all the neighborhood, or a goodly company of them come together by tolling of the bell, and carry the dead solemnly to his grave, and then stand by him while he is buried. The ministers are most commonly present.*[130]

Little had changed by the time the aforementioned Joshua Hempstead kept his diary. Hempstead was an active man in the town of New London, Connecticut, serving in a variety of capacities, including as a guardian for some widows in the town. He was a faithful worshipper and active citizen at the meetinghouse and used his skills as a carpenter to shingle the building, make repairs and construct new pews as well. Among the services he provided to the community were toolmaking, home and barn repairs and the construction of coffins for those who died during the course of the year.

The winter of 1711–12, in particular, kept Hempstead busy with this task, as well as attending funerals and sometimes helping oversee them when deacons and ministers themselves became ill. During the period from late November into mid-December, Hempstead's *Diary* provides a grim view of daily life and death in the colonial town.

> *Sun. 9th…Mr. Neast died yesterday (,) was buried today. One of Jno Tinker's died to day infant. Capt. Morgan of Groaton died yesterday. Mon. 10th…I*

went into ye woods to Split wood thence to Uncle Fox's to see John he being very sick. Mr. Adams was there also & many of ye neighbors (harris from R. Isle att night) I watched with him.…Tues. 11ᵗʰ I was with John Fox all day he was very ill. I stayed with him all night also.…Wed. 12ᵗʰ…I was at Uncle Fox's all day. John died about 10 O'clock morn. I came to town to get my tools to make a coffin and begin itt. I lay there all night. Thurs. 17ᵗʰ Fair. I finished Jno Fox's coffin: I stayed for the funeral. A windy cold day.[131]

Scarcely more than a week later, on the twenty-second, Hempstead was called out

in ye morn before daylight…to help lay out Thomas Way Junior who died at Griffins sick but six days. I made his coffin and found bods and nils. Itt snowed a little today.…Ye snow is now nearly 2 ft. Sund, 25ᵗʰ Fair & Cold.…Thos. Way was buried between meetings.

Near the close of the month, two of Hempstead's aunts fell ill, and one expired, thus the earlier entry about retrieving the black cloth. On Monday the thirty-first, just a few days after his aunt's funeral, he was called on while cutting wood and learned that his neighbor John Lester had died. Hempstead spent most of the evening constructing Lester's coffin. He could not have known that in the coming weeks and months, the illness that had taken his acquaintance would decimate a large part of the Lester family in New London.

During the years 1711 through 1716, Hempstead attended thirty-two funerals and constructed the caskets for twenty-one of his neighbors and three relatives, including, heartbreakingly, his own son, who died at the age of seventeen after a measles epidemic swept through town. Hempstead's wife and daughter fell ill as well but survived.

Churches were still few and far between in rural New England communities of the late eighteenth century and often bereft of ministers to fill them.[132] Sometimes the deacons of the church flock would have to conduct services, as Hempstead did. Doctors or physicians were also often called away, and for every person administered to, another waited for their return.

In the diary of Private Noah Robinson, enlisted with Daggat's Regiment of Attleboro, Massachusetts, during part of the Revolutionary War, we find that he was off duty on Tuesday, February 10, 1778, when he

returned home & early in ye evening Mother was suddenly seized extremely ill, so I hurried after Doc Mann but he was not at home so I returned. She

Congregational church, Whitinsville, Massachusetts. *Photo by author.*

being no better, I went after Doc Bliss & he was not at home so she had no doctor till the evening. Doctor (?) came however no relief was found so she remained very bad all night.

Feb. 11, Wed. Last night I dreamt a frightful dream. However early in the morning my father came into the room....He told me that my mother was not like to live long in his opinion, so I rose, and when I saw her face I was persuaded that she was not long for this world. However Doc Mann came & saw her & he said that there could be no help for her and to our sorrow found it so. About 11 o'clock she left this world which caused a lamentable day—but the bereaving hand of God comes without delay.

Thurs, 12ᵗʰ Last night Mr. ASLS set up with the corpse. Aunt Capron & Mrs. Anna also tarried at our house. This morning J. Dagget set off to Warwick to carry my brother the news.…Preparation is making for the funeral tomorrow at 1 o'clock.

Feb. 13ᵗʰ Fri. A day of weeping is now at hand when the neighbors and friends are gathering together to bury the corpse of my poor Mother.[133]

While rural communities still practiced funeral rites much as they had since the early years of their settlement, in urban towns, farewells to the dead were becoming more formalized and ritualized, including the presentation of gifts to those who attended a funeral.

Gifts and Rituals

Gloves were traditionally given to those who served as underbearers and pallbearers—in other words, those who handled the coffin from the meetinghouse or the church to the cemetery. The attending minister also received a pair, which were usually of white, purple or black cloth. The *Boston Independent Advertiser* displayed an ad in 1749 that offered "Black Shammy Gloves and White Glazed Lambs Wool Gloves suitable for funerals."[134]

Early in the eighteenth century, the tradition expanded to sending out gloves and scarves to relatives as an invitation to the funeral, before becoming the popular expectation of all who were invited. Such was the fashion that according to records kept by Andrew Elliot of Boston's North Church, he and his family received 2,940 pairs of gloves over thirty-two years of service as a minister—so many, in fact, that he sold a good number through local milliners and made a considerable profit.

Mourning rings were a popular token of remembrance at the funerals of those prominent and wealthy individuals of town. Originally, such rings were handed out to the relatives and family of the deceased as well as to the minister. These, according to Alice Morse Earle's *Customs and Fashions of Old New England*, were often made of gold and enameled in black or sometimes black and white. They were often decorated with the "death's-head" of a skull adorned by wings or, sometimes, a full-length skeleton in a coffin. The

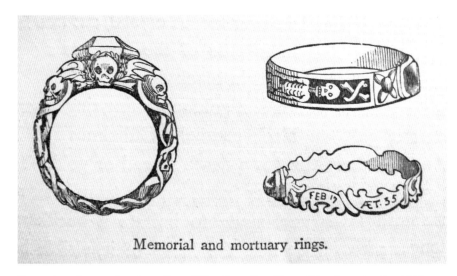

Memorial and mortuary rings.

Illustration of mourning rings. *From William Jones, Esq.*, Finger-Ring Lore *(London, 1890).*

rings were also often embellished with a serpent, from whose mouth came the words that circled the ring: "Be prepared to follow me."

The crafting of memorial or "memory rings" dates to ancient times in both Greece and Egypt and was also prevalent among European and Anglo-Saxon cultures through the Middle Ages into the colonial era. Among those early families settling in New England may have been some who held such tokens among the heirlooms handed down to them and brought with them to New England. I will offer a brief history.

This custom was first almost exclusively kept by royal circles, but as wealth and influence outside the Crown increased, the practice of giving rings to relatives and friends was adapted by the English gentry, who often embellished rings with the family signet or crest. For these men, heritage, upbringing and education were the roots of the pride they upheld through their oversight of vast estates and their social status.

Among the earliest records held in the collection of the Cambridge library are those of physician Jasper Despotin, who in 1648 willed and appointed "ten rings of gold to be made to the value of twenty shillings a peace sterling, with a death's head on some of them, within one moneth after my departure, and to be disposed of among my friends as my Executor shall think meet."[135]

In 1682, Splaker Lenthall appointed his executor "to give my friends Sir John Lenthall, his lady and children, and other [of] my cozens and nephews 50 gold rings with this motto: 'oritur non moritur.'"[136]

Sir Henry Wotten left to each of the fellows at Eton College "a plain gold ring, enameled black, all save the verge, with the motto within 'amor unit omnis.'"[137]

The famous naturalist and fisherman Izaak Walton added a codicil to his 1683 will for the distribution of memorial rings to several of his relatives and friends with the motto: "A friend's farewell. I.W. obit." Walton also had personalized rings made for his son and son-in-law.

In England, the formal practice of giving rings to funeral attendees seems to have been established around 1719.

The practice seems to have entered the culture of early New England by the late seventeenth century. Judge Samuel Sewall of Salem is said to have received fifty-two mourning rings between the years 1687 and 1725. Another prominent individual of Salem was Dr. Samuel Buxton, who on his death in 1758 left his heirs with a quart tankard full of mourning rings.[138]

Goldsmiths kept a constant supply of gold rings on hand, ready for enameling or customizing for patrons. As Alice Morse Earle noted,

> It is very evident that old New Englanders looked with much eagerness to receiving a funeral ring at the death of a friend, and in old diaries, almanacs and note-books, such entries as this are often seen: "Made a ring at the funeral" or "A deaths-head ring made at the funeral of so and so", or, as Judge Sewell wrote, "Lost a ring" by not attending the funeral.[139]

As the expense of funerals became greater, authorities attempted to curb costs. The town of Salem, Massachusetts, limited the fee charged by undertakers to eight shillings and that charged by the sextons to eight pence and stipulated that they must "toll the bell but four strokes a minute."

In 1741, a Massachusetts Provincial Enactment forbade gloves, scarves, rings, wine or rum to be distributed at funerals. A fine of fifty pounds was to be served on violation of the enactment. It was a law that was difficult to enforce, and a telling sign of the stubbornness of the tradition was that in 1767, Boston enacted a law "not to use any mourning gloves but those that are manufactured here."[140] A later attempt to revisit the original enactment reduced the fine to twenty shillings for any individual who distributed gloves, scarves, wine or rum at a funeral.

FUNERAL JEWELRY

As gifts to funeral attendees lessened, the fashion for a jeweled remembrance of the deceased continued among friends and family.

Locks of the hair of the deceased were braided into rings, bracelets and necklaces as well as enclosed in rings, pendants and glass-covered brooches. Pendants bearing monuments and figures of mourning also became popular. The figures in these bas-relief carvings are often touching the monument and holding a hand to their face in an attitude of grief.[141]

All manner of brooches were manufactured for this fashion. Larger brooches with gold trim and enameled bas-relief interiors were made with a glass face like that of a locket, which the wearer could open to insert a curl of hair or other keepsake. The backs of such brooches were usually engraved in memory of the deceased.

Pins of black enamel and gold or silver design with jewels inlaid became popular *memento mori* for grieving families, as did later personalized mourning rings.

MEMORIAL PORTRAITS

While a tradition of deathbed portraits and, later, death masks existed among European rulers and the gentry, the common man might have a "coffin portrait" or likeness of the deceased placed on the funeral bier and kept later by a loved one.

As itinerant painters and artists from Europe visited the colonies, portraits became more accessible, and many took the opportunity to have spouses or other members of the family memorialized on canvas.

With the "imminence of death" in early New England, as art historian Lillian B. Miller has noted, portraits of family members became all the more desirable,

> *especially portraits of women and children. Among the group of family portraits that Roberts sent to Elizabeth Shrimpton in Boston was one of her dying sister Katherine, who died soon after her portrait was taken. "Wee little thought," he wrote to Elizabeth, "ye curtaine would be so soon drawn over yet being intended for you hath sent it yt you may see by ye shadow what a sweet likely babe it to live."...*

The portrait of Elizabeth Eggington (1664: Wadsworth Athenaeum, Hartford, Connecticut), Cotton Mather's niece, was presumably taken after her death to retain her likeness for her absent seafaring father.

These, and probably other family portraits, testify to the concern of families to retain likenesses of departed members as well as to the realistic recognition—taught at an early age to New England children in such texts as The New England Primer (1727)—that "Youth forward slips, Death soonest nips."[142]

The craft of needlework being taught to young girls in colonial houses sometimes wrought memorial portraits beyond the country scenes of home and garden that adorned most needlework of the period. Mourning scenes began to be produced as early as 1804 and often depicted family members visiting the graves of the deceased. As the form progressed, the typical scene would include the gravestone or crypt; a willow beside it, branches draped over the stone; and perhaps one or two mourners.

Early folk art paintings by itinerant artists began to portray funerals as they did other family gatherings. These commissioned or family-painted landscapes preserved a moment of family history that was personalized just as the traditional picnics and weddings that were the more common subjects of this genre of American painting.

Several of the early "lumineers" or folk artists of New England became quite popular for these mourning portraits, which had become a common form during the nineteenth century. Indeed, in the headlong days of the early republic, lumineers were among the thousands of itinerant craftsmen plying their trade. As historian David Jaffe writes,

Obtaining their artistic training from the pages of design books or from brief encounters with other untrained painters, portraitists traversed the countryside creating images that range from stark black and white silhouettes to colorful, full-length oils.... These family portraits found a ready market among "middling" craftsmen, innkeepers, and farmers who sought symbols of middle-class identity and belonging.[143]

Among the earliest of these limners were young men like Nehemiah Partridge from Portsmouth, New Hampshire. He first appeared as a japanner, or decorative artist, in Boston around 1712, and later, having been introduced to society circles in Albany, New York, he was commissioned by several families before traveling on to Newport, Rhode Island, and Jamestown

Example of "mourning picture," artist and date unknown. *Courtesy of Wikimedia Commons.*

and Williamsburg, Virginia. For many years, his work went unattributed; he signed his paintings with the Latin phrase "Aetatis Saue Limner" followed by the sitter's age and the date of composition. A discovery by art historian Mary Black in a patron's daybook would lead to the identification of some eighty portraits painted in his hand.[144]

Later artists included J. Brown, who traveled the Berkshires painting portraits from 1806 to 1808, and Ammi Phillips of Kent, Connecticut, who in 1809 embarked on a long and fruitful career among families within the triangle of the Connecticut, New York and Massachusetts border region. The posthumous portrait of a family member was among his most common commissions. In the painter's journal of 1857, he expresses gratitude at receiving word of one family's response to his efforts: "Lenny's portrait came tonight. Mother and even Father is perfectly satisfied with it. I was so thankful—it will be a comfort and it will mean more than anything else in the world to us, now."[145]

Other artists like Chester Harding and Rufus Porter succeeded in refining their skills in portraiture over long careers. Women also, especially those who were gifted in the "schoolgirl arts," adapted their skills to include portraiture.

Mary Way was an early pioneer among women itinerant painters. The prolific Ruth Pinney, from a well-to-do family of Simsbury, Connecticut, became known for her genre scenes, mourning pictures and illustrations from literary sources—all common subjects in schools and academies, though as she "learned her palette in the Eighteenth century," she relied more on her own extensive research and her familiarity with English prints.[146]

Women artists such as Ruth Henshaw Bacom and Deborah Goldsmith continued the craft until the advent of the daguerreotype and, ultimately, the grim and macabre practice of death portraits in Victorian America, in which the family sat with the dead dressed and propped up as though still living among them.

Later tintype photographs included family portraits with the matriarch or patriarch of the family propped upright in the casket for the family to gather around. These most commonly were taken at the wake of the deceased, usually inside the parlor, but I have even seen some of these scenes arranged outdoors, seemingly on the steps of a church or at the entrance to the family home.

As odd as it may seem to us now, I recently heard the somewhat startling statement that the purportedly most popular use of Polaroid instant cameras in the late twentieth century was to take a final picture of the deceased in the casket at their funeral.

SHROUDS, COFFINS AND CASKETS

Those who were among the first to die in the settlements of New England were buried in shrouds made from what was known as cerecloth, or linen coated in wax. Wool shrouds were also used, often dipped in alum or pitch. These were sewn carefully with a drawstring at the top to tie them closed. This form of burial most likely originally carried from the tradition of wrapping those who had died at sea in sailcloth before committing them to the deep.

The first coffins, as the reader may have noted from Joshua Hempstead's diary, were made of plain pine and constructed as soon as possible after word was sent of the individual's death. These were simple rectangular boxes or "cellar-doors," six-sided coffins and lids.[147] Traditionally, the wood shavings from the construction of the coffin were placed inside as a bed for the corpse. While these early coffins were most commonly made of pine and unadorned with handles, it was the tradition in northern states of New England to paint the coffin, often with an ochre or a dried ox-blood powder mixed with fish oil to better soak into the wood.

As the eighteenth century progressed, materials became more varied and available to those who could afford this luxury for their departed. Walnut, cherry, poplar and mahogany were popular choices by the early nineteenth century. The finished coffin was now varnished or rubbed with beeswax and polished, and the interior was now lined with muslin or some other cloth. A glass viewing window was sometimes part of the lid, or a piece of the lid might be removed for viewing or slid down inside the coffin for the same.

As local craftsman became more engaged for this service, village country stores began stocking accessories that enabled the local carpenter or cabinetmaker to "dress up" the coffin for customers. These included sets of brass handles, elongated steel tacks, heavy brass screws, cross-shaped nails and metal plates made of brass, silver, copper or tin. These were often engraved with a loving phrase or simply the name of the deceased.[148]

Coffins began to be mass manufactured as early as 1812. These early versions offered to the public were often lead-lined, eliminating the need for the outer, tin-lined box that the coffin was once lowered into at the grave site. Within another twenty years, multiple patent applications for the manufacture of coffins made from marble, stone, cast iron and cement illustrated the growing industry of funerary services.[149] The modern-shaped "casket" as we know it today was not manufactured until the second half of the nineteenth century when a Connecticut carpenter named William Smith began making rectangular burial boxes with perpendicular sides.[150]

THE FIRST HEARSES

The long tradition of funeral processions would also eventually be regulated. Such processions were forbidden on Sunday in Massachusetts, and selectmen were chosen to keep a calendar of such processions so that "free passage in the streets could be kept open."[151]

The first hearses were little more than funeral biers outfitted with wheels. As the village cemeteries began to fill, land on the edge of town was acquired

Early horse-drawn funeral bier. *Courtesy of Plymouth Courthouse Museum.*

and the distance for pallbearers to carry a coffin became too far. While in rural communities, a neighbor's wagon would be borrowed to draw the coffin to the grave on a bed of straw, the more formal undertakers, in the towns and cities in particular, began to introduce horse-drawn hearses that would provide a more dignified procession for their customers.

According to Margaret M. Coffin's *Death in Early America*,

> *The early horse-drawn hearses would appear fragile to us today, the chassis teetering on high springs and spindly wheels. Some were about the size of the old tin peddlers cart, with a door at the back and only one compartment. There was a roller on the rear floor to ease the coffin in and out, and open windows on the sides, often three....The first hearses had no glass in the windows, some had woolen draperies or fringe curtains with tassels. Although the chassis of these vehicles were plain, there were apt to be ornaments on the top, a series of urns, or black draped torches....The driver sat on a box attached to the front with no roof overhead.*[152]

Coffin also informs us that while hearses made for adults were always black, those constructed to be used in the funerals of infants were often painted white and sometimes blue. Her book contains a photo of a small, egg-shaped hearse for an infant's coffin.

Elegant nineteenth-century hearse. *Courtesy of the Portsmouth Historical Society.*

Later hearses were more elaborate and elegant, often having a large viewing window bedecked with black lace curtains and bunting. These great carriages would be drawn by two or as many as four horses driven by a mortician in a black coat and top hat. An entourage of elegant and plain carriages and chaises would follow in what was now a more stately procession to the graveyard.

Minister Ezra Stiles of Newport recorded multiple funerals in his diary from 1769 through the end of the century. One particular funeral that likely had such a hearse was held on January 26, 1772, as he recorded:

At V P.M. my Wife and I attended the Funeral of Billy Marchant *who died yesterday at three years, only son of our worthy Friend Mr. Agent Marchant in London. The Funeral proceeded in fifteen chaises. Mrs. Marchant fainted at the grave. He cometh forth like a flower and is cut down.*[153]

The Burial Ground

The places of burial also evolved over the years. As colonial towns increased in size, more impressive stone and brick churches began to be constructed, and as was the custom in England, the ministers and deacons who served there and the more prominent members of the parish began to be entombed beneath the churches themselves. In one Boston church, it was even possible to be buried beneath the family pew for an extra fee.[154]

The common parishioners came to be buried in plots of land adjacent to the church or sometimes in a field across the road bequeathed or purchased for that purpose. Such cemeteries inevitably grew beyond the simple plots designated by the parish, city or town for such use. Even then, the spiritual connection sought by the living with the dead was an integral part of the community's existence.

Again in Margaret M. Coffin's work, we find that as early as Puritan times, burial grounds were important public spaces. Burial grounds adjacent to meetinghouses and churchyards became places to picnic and ponder the messages carved on the gravestones between services on the Sabbath.

Less populated settlements often designated areas at the edge of town or in places that were less likely to be populated. One of the oldest of these lies on a hill within the limits of Charlestown, Massachusetts. The site is bordered by an estuary of the Charles River on one side and was originally flanked by marshlands to the south and west. It was designated as the town burial ground in 1630. Among the earliest interred were veterans of the various conflicts with Indigenous people and soldiers slain in King Philip's War. Among those buried there are Thomas Beecher, an early settler in the Massachusetts Bay Colony, as well as John Harvard and his family. The graves of all those prominent families of Charlestown—including the Frothinghams, the aforementioned Harvard family, the Hurds, the Hunnewells and the Phipps and Russell families—are to be found in their original configuration within what has long been known as the Phipps Street Cemetery.[155]

The first cemetery in the city of Boston was recorded to be the garden plot of Isaac Johnson, one of the town's first settlers. Johnson built a small house on a plot of land that lay on the corner of the present School and Tremont Streets. He was an avid gardener and, as he grew older, often expressed his wish to be buried within his vegetable plot. When he died in 1630, he was duly interred in the southwest corner of his garden.

Lithograph of the Ballou Meeting House. *Courtesy of the Blackstone Valley Historical Society.*

View of Ballou Meeting House Cemetery. *Photo by author.*

For the next thirty years, the town lay its dead in this small plot, from the illustrious to the poorest citizen. In 1688, the newly appointed governor, Sir Andross, confiscated the plot of land and erected the colony's First Episcopal Church, thereafter known as Kings Chapel, and the small burial place became the town's first churchyard.[156]

An early burial ground in Newtowne (later called Cambridge) lay on the south side of Brattle Street adjacent to present Longfellow Parl. However, the site had no protection from wild animals and was soon abandoned.

The Old Burial Ground in Cambridge was set aside in 1635 and initially contained but an acre of land. More common land was added to the parcel, and the construction of Christ Church in 1760 consolidated both the lane of Garden Street and the western boundary of the cemetery. In 1833, the First Parish Church was erected on the eastern boundary.

The burial ground served as the only common resting place for Cambridge citizens for over two hundred years, and within its expansive grounds between the two churches lie stone tributes to both the privileged and the poor. The oldest stone still in existence dates from 1635 and belongs to one Anne Erinton, though it may have been added later after carved stones became the preferred adornment for a family member's resting place.

Several large burial vaults also lie within the cemetery grounds, including the John Vassal family vault, which came to contain twenty-five caskets, including that of Andrew Carnegie, who had purchased the Vassal estate, as well as the family pew at Christ Church and burial rights in the vault.

The Old Burial Ground also contains the graves of Revolutionary War soldiers and active citizens, including the three White revelers killed in the Boston Massacre of April 1775 as well as the enslaved men of color Neptune Frost and Cato Stedman.

Many urban dwellers, however, long followed the custom of their rural relations and preferred to bury their dead in a family plot on their own property. In Providence, Rhode Island, this practice dated to the time of founder Roger Williams's death in 1683, when he was interred between his vegetable garden and orchard on the hillside where his home lay above the river.

Those who died intestate were buried in a corner of a common lot about a mile from the "compact part of town,"[157] a site that had been used as a commons for some years on which citizens could graze their cattle and sheep. Conveniently for these farmers, a tavern was established by Jacob Mowry nearby.

A small corner of the common area had also been used for a burial ground long before the settlement of the town, and the graves of those in the city

View of North Burial Ground, Providence, Rhode Island. *Photo by author.*

who had died in intestate or indigent were added to the Indigenous graves that occupied the site.

In 1700, the town of Providence officially designated this site, as part of a forty-five-acre parcel of the common, as the first burial ground for the community. The first formal interments did not occur until a decade after its designation, and the North Burial Ground, as it became known, would in the coming years add many of the town's citizens who had remained undisturbed in family plots until additions to their houses, the sale of land or other development caused them to be removed.

The North Burial Ground also became the chosen resting place of several colonial-era governors, Revolutionary War heroes and average citizens who lived and worked in the seaside community.

By the 1840s, however, the burial ground had become unkempt, the grounds a camping area for destitute citizens and the sepulchers often broken into and damaged by fires in winter.

During that decade, a committee formed by Zachariah Allen set out to improve the burial ground. By 1845, surveyors Atwater & Schubarth had begun construction on their design to transform the burial ground into a garden cemetery.

The Age of the Garden Cemetery

By the early nineteenth century, the longstanding practice of burying the dead in underground vaults beneath a church or in the now-crowded adjacent plots of land began to be viewed as unhealthy for the living inhabitants near such burial places. Medical doctors especially began to promote this view. One Dr. Buchan wrote an epistle in 1850 that would be broadly published in New England newspapers, which read, in part,

> *It is very common in this country to have churchyards in the middle of populous cities. Certain it is, that thousands of putrid carcasses, so near the surface of the earth in a place where the air is confined, cannot fail to taint it; and that such air, when breathed into the lungs must occasion diseases.*[158]

That the practice of entombing people beneath the churches themselves was still common alarmed the doctor even more, as places of worship "are seldom open above once a week, are never ventilated by fires nor open windows, and rarely kept clean. This occasions that damp, musty, unwholesome smell…and renders it a very unsafe place for the living."[159]

In 1825, Boston physician and Harvard Medical School professor Joseph Bigelow convened a committee of notable citizens to search for a site for a spacious, natural cemetery whose beauty would relieve the common burial ground's vista of row after row of gravestones on the landscape. With an interest in both architecture and horticulture beyond his medical profession, Bigelow also served as the secretary of the Massachusetts Horticultural Society.

The committee surveyed several sites; one in Brookline was deemed too expensive, but a section of the old Simon Stone farm in Watertown, dating from 1635, included a prominent ridge with a level summit that sat 125 feet above the river with a panoramic view of the city and its neighboring countryside.[160]

A Boston merchant named George Brimmer had acquired much of the Stone farm between 1828 and 1831 and, at this time, agreed to sell seventy-two acres of the property to the Massachusetts Horticultural Society for use as a cemetery and "experimental garden."

Another of the society's members, General Dearborn, took charge of laying out the roadwork and the grounds. According to a history of the cemetery, Dearborn "hoe in hand, day after day"[161] led the laborers in creating and laying out what is generally acknowledged to be the finest garden cemetery of its time in New England. Aside from the later leveling

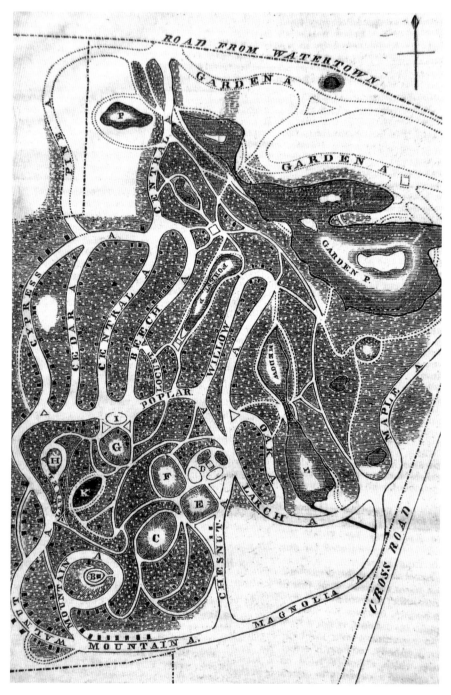

Finished map of Jacob Bigelow's landscape design for Mount Auburn Cemetery. *Alexander Wadsworth, 1833.*

of a few small hills and the filling in of marshlands, the lay of the beautiful Mount Auburn Cemetery remains much as Dearborn and his workers landscaped the park in the 1830s.

Other New England communities began to create their own landscaped burial grounds. The setting for what would become the Mount Hope Garden Cemetery of Bangor, Maine, began with the purchase of fifty acres that contained the highest point of land above the town to be named Cemetery Hill,

> *which overlooked a large turn in the Penobscot such that one could see the river and countryside from multiple directions, in addition to a number of smaller undulations on the landscape, each of which would contribute to the beauty of the cemetery.*[162]

Local architect George G. Bryant designed the overall layout of the cemetery, but the committee itself tackled the progressive tasks of laying out a road to the site; deciding on the trees, shrubs, flora and fauna to plant in selected locations; and placing walls and fencing where needed. The cemetery was officially dedicated on July 21, 1836.

A decade later, the town of Providence, Rhode Island, allowed speculators to fill in a semi-wooded area long known as the "Cat-Swamp" and create an entirely new landscape with trees, shrubbery and footpaths that initially covered some sixty acres. Swan Point Cemetery would become the repository of many memorial sculptures and monuments and remains a fine, meticulously preserved example of the era that still inters citizens today.

Landscaped, parklike cemeteries continued to grow in popularity and in scope and would become sites of poignant Civil War memorials and, in the Victorian age, the more elaborate memorials constructed for those families who grew wealthy in the industrial age.

By the mid-nineteenth century, the longstanding rural practice of burying the dead in a family plot on the property was also beginning to wane. Families who could afford the expense had their ancestors' remains removed to new, parklike, communal cemeteries as they began to grow. Those old cemeteries left behind, usually in a far-flung corner of a pasture or beneath a grove of trees, were left to become overgrown, and as acreage was sold off, they were forgotten and often "fell by way of the plow."

This was especially true of those slave cemeteries that were further removed from houses. Often, when family remains were transported, the graves of the servants of the household were left behind.

Ellis family plot, now part of the Tillinghast Pond Preserve, West Greenwich, Rhode Island. *Photo by author.*

View of Swan Point Cemetery, Providence, Rhode Island. *Photo by author.*

Many of these forgotten family and enslaved lots were recorded to be in a run-down and overgrown condition by James N. Arnold and George J. Harris in the 1880s as they compiled the first farm-by-farm survey of private cemeteries in the region of South County, Rhode Island. These surveys would come to be especially useful to the Rhode Island Genealogical Society's efforts to update the status of these historic cemeteries in South Kingstown, Exeter, Westerly, Newport, Warwick and Providence as they published their own surveys a century or more later.

In the spring of 1880, Harris recorded a description of the Willett-Carpenter slave lot:

> *On a knoll a few rods south west from the Carpenter Burial Ground on opposite side of road in an open lot and unprotected is a burial yard containing 10 graves we are told were slaves of the Willet and Carpenter families. Whither there were more graves we know not though the plow has run fearfully close.*[163]

The "mystery" skull that appeared in local newspapers in 1901, found amid the remains of a stone wall removed by roadworkers in the farming community of Johnston, Rhode Island, was likely that of an early laborer on the property, and the farmer who inadvertently dug up the cranium hid the skull within the wall that bordered his newly plowed field.

Communal burial sites for rural populations began as in urban areas, with a plot beside or close by the meetinghouse, which, in early years, was some distance from inhabitants. The picturesque scene of a New England common surrounded by the town house, tavern, a pair of churches, etc. did not evolve until the nineteenth century. While the meetinghouse and commons might be close by one another, the commons was used as a grazing ground for cattle and sheep and the meetinghouse all but abandoned during the week until Sabbath-day services.

The town of Durham, Connecticut, provides a fine example. The town green was established in 1707 but looked far different from the clover-filled swath of lawn the visitor finds today. The site was originally fenced in and "haywards" appointed to keep the fences in good repair. A meetinghouse was constructed along with a set of stables. The early "town green" then was "probably more dirt than grass, due to the constant traffic of humans, horses, and the hogs and geese the town allowed to run free."[164]

The town cemetery lay just down Durham Road, and when the lot near the road was filled, it expanded up the hillside as graves were added. The

Town Cemetery, Durham, Connecticut. *Photo by author.*

cemetery dates from 1700 and includes at least one memorial, that of Timothy Hall, among the victims of a smallpox epidemic whose remains were actually buried in unmarked graves on the grounds of a pesthouse in the shadow of nearby Mount Pisgah.[165]

As the nineteenth century waned, the expansion of public parks replaced the notion that burial places need be the only source of experiencing nature. Many of those planners who would create some of the finest parks in New England would borrow ideas from those garden cemeteries they visited. Burial sites became an expanded version of the Puritan churchyards: lawn cemeteries that would become landscapes of neatly lined tombstones rather than sculpted monuments and designed family plots with grid-like roads rather than winding paths. Individual gravestones then became of more importance in their outward expression of the deceased's life or personality, whether by the choice of stone, the shape in which it was cut or the design on its face.

CHAPTER 6

EARLY GRAVESTONES AND
THE MEN WHO CARVED THEM

E arly memorials to the dead were simple monuments, a wooden cross or slab with a name and date, nothing that would last beyond the lives of those who knew the deceased. To leave a more lasting memorial, they believed, would be vanity.

Not all early settlers were bound by such constraints. While this early period held few professional stone carvers, those who created memorials left the small boulders with, at times, just initials and a date that we find in early New England cemeteries. Later memorials would be upright headstones made from "a slab of slate, schist, marble, limestone, greenstone, granite, micha stone, or red or brown sandstone."[166]

Once the stone carver of the community was given the task of carving a stone, he first hauled the stone by horse on a sled called a "stone boat," often used in removing boulders from ploughed fields. After hauling the stone to his shop, he would cut it using a drill and sledge.

A gravestone would then be cut from this piece with a toothless saw. The carver's most popular choice of stone was slate, because as it forms in layers, it is relatively easily split to the desired width of the slab.

The stone carver would then cut the requested design with a small chisel and mallet. A more skilled carver might sculpt the stone itself, creating a bas-relief portrait and a border of leaves for his customer.[167]

Another early type of monument was a large slab called a "wolf-stone" that covered the ground above a family burial site. The stone bore the names of the family's deceased relations, added to over time, with the

Elegant box tombs in the Casey family plot. *Courtesy of Historic New England.*

coffin below, protected from wolves or other scavengers that plagued early New England farms.

Later memorials evolved from this in the manner of "box monuments," where the slab would be lifted from the ground by a stone foundation and a layer of bricks.

A glimpse into materials used and the cost of these memorials may be found in the account book of John Stevens, an early Newport stone carver. Stevens opened his shop in 1705, in what was then the most prosperous city in the colony of Rhode Island. As historian John E. Sterling has pointed out, Stevens was the "first resident carver in Newport…and progressed rapidly from crude relief work to wonderful and distinctive carving."[168]

As with other early carvers, Stevens's skill was one of many he owned and carving stones just one of his many labors. Stevens made shoes, built chimneys and stairways, plastered and whitewashed walls and carved firestone hearths.

Once established, his shop was increasingly productive and profitable. As Sterling writes, "The Stevens shop carved small children's gravestones in about three days and charged £1 10s. Larger adult gravestones took six to eight days and were charged £3–£4."[169]

Box tombs for wealthier clients, as described earlier, cost between twelve and fifty-seven pounds, depending on the size and complexity of carving desired. A coat of arms, for instance, took up to eleven days to finish. A pair of these instances are notable in the account book. In 1726, Stevens received an order for an elaborate box tomb from the merchant George Wanton. Grief-stricken at the loss of his young wife, Abigail, Wanton ordered the carving of the family coat of arms, as well as a 528-letter epitaph to be carved into the large slab. The cost for the memorial came to twenty pounds, eight shillings.

Another account lists the cost and materials used for the grave of former governor William Brenton. The costly tomb was ordered by the governor's son Jalel Brenton when he was in his later years so that he could commemorate his father, who had died in 1674. The order would be the most expensive item in the shop account book, and Stevens carefully itemized the bill:

Mr. Jalel Brenton 1727

	L	S	P
One double tombstone for the Governor	45	00	00
600 bricks at six shillings a hundred	01.	16.	00
Lime 11 bushels	00.	13.	00
Sand bushels at 6 a bushel	00.	04.	00
Two stones for the foundation	00	08.	00
Carting the bricks and lime and sand	00.	07.	00
Carting the tombstone	01.	00.	00
Cutting the coate of arms	05.	10.	00
Bilding ye boxes	02.	10.	00

The total cost was fifty-seven pounds, eight shillings and nine pence.

Early ornamentation on gravestones included grimacing skulls and crossbones; skeletons, sometimes encased in their coffins; or hourglasses whose sand had run down. These motifs remained popular from the time of the Puritan burial grounds to about 1700.

The eighteenth century ushered in the far less grim and more delicate work of winged cherubs, angels and early bas-relief portraits of the dead carved on gravestones. So well-known did the craftsmanship of some carvers in the region become throughout this era that examples of their work can be found in almost all the early New England burial grounds as well as in New York State.

In his essay "The Carvers of Kingston, Massachusetts," professor James Blachowicz notes several notable carvers who produced work for the

Tombstone of John Greene, 1726, carved by Henry Emmes. *Photo by author.*

communities of southern New England. They also wandered, nomad-like, and worked occasionally as itinerant carvers as they sought a community in which to establish their own business. "The resident gravestone carving tradition of the town of Plymouth, Massachusetts began in 1770," Blachowicz writes, "with the arrival of William Coye from Providence, Rhode Island."[170]

Within the next decade, several other carvers had begun work in the county. Among the first was Bildad Washburn, who began work under the tutelage of Lemuel Savery, an early Plymouth carver. He opened his own shop in Kingston around 1777, and among his early carvings are the grim winged skull stones that can be found in Kingston's Old Burial Ground.[171]

Washburn married Lucy Adams in 1784, and they established a home and tavern on Main Street, purchasing an existing house in Marshfield, dismantling it and moving the parts by packet ship and oxcart to the chosen location. He and his wife would raise fourteen children. In 1798, Washburn paid a hefty fee at auction for a pew in the new meetinghouse. He would serve as town clerk from 1804 to 1806.

The stonecutter taught two of his sons, Alvan and Elias, the craft of stonecutting and took on Bartlett Adams, his wife's brother, as an apprentice when he came of age. Within the next decade, Adams set up his own shop in

Portland, Maine. The Washburns and Adamses continued working together, Alvan working in the Portsmouth shop while Bartlett Adams produced work in Charlestown. Later, in 1818, Washburn's younger son, Elias, would apprentice in Adams's shop.

Between them, the two shops produced an estimated 489 stones, 376 carved by Washburn's shop, 113 by Adams, 11 of those in Portland. During Adams's time as an apprentice in Kingston, the Washburn shop also produced stones for towns north of Kingston, such as Brockton, and for Milton, Massachusetts.

Washburn's most popular motif was a smiling, infant-faced cherub whose head was topped by a carefully coiffed wig and whose wings, rising symmetrically on either side of the face, were carefully detailed as well, with feathers and a lacelike scroll around the edges.

Early Washburn-like wigged angel motif, Burial Hill, Plymouth, Massachusetts. *Photo by author.*

Adams also carved cherubs and, as an apprentice, copied Washburn's model of a childlike cherub. However, once an established carver on his own, his style developed quite differently and distinctly from that of his mentor: "The cherubs on these stones have a more pointed chin as well as diverse hair styles—straight, wavy, a forelock combed back, combed forward. Further, there are additional decorative features above the cherub's head."[172] Typically, Washburn's winged cherubs took up the entirety of the upper stone.

The two carvers also produced stones with large and small urns on them, the larger typically carved in bas-relief to hold the name of the deceased, dates of birth and death and a brief epitaph. The urn was usually in the shadow of a leafy willow, whose branches reached down just above or to partially cover the urn.

Stones with smaller urns usually were carved as other stones: the decorative motif was carved onto the crest of the stone, be it curved, square or pointed. A similar motif occurs on other stones, with a more distinctly carved urn, shadowed by a highly detailed willow tree.

Washburn also experimented with carving bas-relief portraits of individuals on commissioned stones later in his career.

Another early carving family of Plymouth County was the Tribbles. John Tribble and his son Winslow produced stones in the early nineteenth century. Hiram Tribble was John's nephew and joined the family shop as an apprentice sometime around 1820. He later moved to Brewster on Cape Cod and worked as an apprentice there in the shop of Ebenezer S. Winslow. While there, he began carving and signing his own stonework; his first stones on the Cape date from 1830. It was a brief sojourn, however, for two years later, he returned to Kingston and joined the Washburn shop. He settled into a house on Summer Street, with his shop just down the road, which included a windmill to power the marble-cutting saws.

Some 340 gravestones are attributed to Hiram Tribble, the majority around his base of Kingston. These include stones he carved while working in Washburn's shop.

Like Adams, once on his own, Tribble began adding some distinctive signatures to his carvings. One of his early designs was a small urn, half concealed by the draped branches of the familiar willow tree. Carved within the base of the urn, however, was a small heart. This signature heart would find its way into Tribble's other designs but remained primarily used as a decorative motif for the base of an urn or pedestal. These mostly date from 1832 to 1833 and can be found in burial grounds in both Plymouth and Kingston, Massachusetts.[173]

As with John Stevens in Newport, Tribble may have continued to carry on the trades learned in his uncle's shop of painting and glazing, as he was listed as a "painter" while also working as a stonecutter in Kingston.

Other Massachusetts stone carvers included John New of Wrentham, who had become well known by the mid-eighteenth century for his especially ornate stones created for wealthy clients on the South Shore. His work is found throughout the Bay Colony, though his most famous sculptures may be of Dr. Thomas Munroe of Bristol, Rhode Island, whose memorial is a life-sized sculpture dressed in peruke, frills and jacket, and the more delicate portrait that adorns the gravestone of Sarah Tyler in Barrington, Rhode Island.

Family-run businesses also flourished in the Massachusetts Bay Colony, with the Soules in Brookfield, the Lamsons in Charlesfield, the Fosters in Dorchester and the Worcesters of Harvard practicing the stone-carving trade in their communities. Individual carvers, such as William Parkham, Henry Christian Geyer, John Gand and William Mumford, worked in the area of Boston.[174]

Soloman Ashley, a carver in the community of Deerfield, contributed many of the gravestones found among private family plots in the village and elsewhere, especially the Old Burying Ground. His signature designs were a slanted "*1*" on each appropriate date carved on the stone and abstract, anthropomorphic figures.[175] Ashley was born and raised in Deerfield, and he and his immediate family share a family plot among the many stones he carved for others in the Old Burying Ground.

Another prolific carver was George Allen, who arrived in Rehoboth from England as a young schoolteacher and became a member of the Congregational Church. It was there that he began carving gravestones for parishioners buried in the churchyard, and by the 1730s, he had sufficient commissions to work almost entirely as a stone carver. He became proficient in producing charming, bald-headed, winged effigies for gravestones and, with his son Gabriel, received 350 commissions for gravestones in Providence's Old North Burial Ground.

Vincent Luti, certainly the foremost among authorities in the stone carvers of New England, would write of Allen:

His extraordinary skill as a draughtsman and carver led to grave and tombstones richly conceived and ornamented with cherubs flying, angels, extremely tilted heads, intricate tracery, heraldic shields, and sorrowing mothers. All but the Newport carvers in the Narragansett basin were influenced by his work.[176]

Top: Early example of Gabriel Allen's stern-faced angel, Burial Hill, Plymouth, Massachusetts. *Photo by author.*

Bottom: Later example of Allen's angel, Ballou Meeting House Cemetery, Cumberland, Rhode Island. *Photo by author.*

Allen's sons also worked in the trade. George Allen Jr. worked briefly in his father's shop during the 1760s but afterward abandoned the craft. His effigies often bear a bemused expression, and his lettering, like his father's, was considered exceptionally well done.

Gabriel Allen was the more prolific carver, working chiefly from the 1770s through 1800. He limited himself to two basic designs, a severe-looking winged effigy or an adorable cherub, complete with bangs hanging over the forehead and a winsome smile. He also excelled in a "peeking sun" design that he carved on a number of gravestones.

Thomas Tingley settled in the town of Attleboro in 1723 and was an early stone carver in that community. He apprenticed his son Samuel, who would be listed as a marble cutter in the town census from the time he reached adulthood. Father and son crafted many stones for what is now South Attleboro but also for the North Burial Ground in Providence, where their cherubs, floral borders and rising sun motifs adorn many gravestones.

The Tingley shop worked predominately with slate, using a smooth, light-colored rock for gravestones in Boston and a green-tinged slate for markers in the Plymouth and Bristol burying grounds. The family was also the first in the region to use limestone, hauling the rock from quarries to their sawmill in South Attleboro.

By 1811, Samuel Tingley's grandsons had moved to Providence, Rhode Island. The 1837 directory of the city shows three members of the family having shops within its boundaries: Samuel Jr. operated a stonecutting shop at 18 Benefit Street, while Silvanus and Edward Tingley are listed as having shops at 68 and 83 South Main Street, respectively. Gravestones signed "S. Tingley & Son" may be found in the city's Old North Burial Ground as well as the churchyard of the Newman Congregational Church in Rumford, Rhode Island, and as far removed as Saunderstown, where their large, carefully scripted headstones for siblings Wanton Casey (1842) and Elizabeth (Goodale) Casey (1830) stand amid the other gravestones of the Casey family.

After their apprenticeship with their father, Henry and John Stevens began working the craft in Boston but removed to Newport, as did Henry Emmes, who held a reputation as one of the most talented carvers in the city. After establishing himself in Newport sometime after 1758, he produced a number of notable stones, including those in the small Greene family plot in Warwick, Rhode Island, settled on a hillside overlooking Occupawtuxet Cove. A grimacing skull and crossbones is carved into the 1762 gravestone of John Greene, while a winsome angel smiles from Elizabeth Greene's gravestone.

Whimsical angel on the tombstone of Elizabeth Greene, Warwick, Rhode Island. *Photo by author.*

Once reestablished in Newport, John Steven's sons, John Jr., Philip and William, would achieve more artistic and monetary success than John Sr. would achieve in his lifetime.

John Stevens Jr.'s elegant winged effigies and delicate styling influenced many carvers of the period. Some of his more intricate designs may be found throughout the region, such as the hourglass enclosed by a scrolled, floral design on the gravestone of Elizabeth Avery in North Stonington, Connecticut, or the twin solemn-faced cherubs carved below a flower bud for the sons of Captain Joshua Belcher in Newport and the crest with three birds surrounded by an intricate foliate design on the stone of Sarah Harris in Providence, Rhode Island's North Burial Ground.

Philip Stevens lived only briefly, murdered at the age of thirty, but his influence on carvers in Connecticut, where his gravestones were usually shipped, gave him the reputation of producing work of great originality and beauty.

William Stevens created his own unique style as well, even incorporating native Rhode Island corn within the borders of his stones. Under his

Tombstone of Sarah Harris, carved by John Stevens Jr. North Burial Ground, Providence, Rhode Island. *Photo by author.*

leadership, the manufacturing of stones was greatly increased, and the Stevens shop held the widest distribution of any of the Newport carvers.

John Bull was a contemporary of the Stevens brothers, having apprenticed under William from the age of fifteen, but apparently displayed a willful independence in both life and work. The stones produced under his apprenticeship, with their look of "wild, bold, large gestured folk art," were installed in the Walker-Blake cemetery of Taunton, Massachusetts, rather than for clients in staid Newport.

Bull ran away to sea, participated in a mutiny, returned to Newport to marry Ruth Cornell of Middletown on August 18, 1769, and had settled for good in Newport by 1775, as advertised, "in the house formerly improved by James Phillips where any person may be supplied with Tomb or Gravestones of the best black slate."[177]

The work of John Bull often resembles the style of William Stevens, but he seems to have had a freer hand with the faces of his effigies, which bear a lifelike quality that is missing from those of his mentor. A few examples of this trait may be seen in the portraits that adorn the gravestones of Benjamin

Wyatt (1767), Nathaniel Coggeshall Jr. (1784), Charles Bardin (1773), Freelove Sophie Rogers (1786) and Hannah Stevens (1791) in Newport's Common Burying Ground.

Bull's work may also be found in Connecticut and New York cemeteries. Bull continued to carve well into his old age; he died on November 28, 1808, leaving his son Henry to carve the stone that was placed on his grave. The son was not nearly as prolific and seems to have abandoned the trade a few years after his father's death.

A well-known carver in Bristol, Rhode Island, was William Throop, originally a tanner in the seaside town. Throop began carving shortly before the Revolutionary War, possibly as an apprentice in the Stevens shop. He served as a captain in Cook's militia during the war and seems to have opened his own shop on his return to Bristol.

Throop's early work is said to have been influenced by John New of Attleboro, though he developed a distinctive effigy of his own. His work was described by a contemporary historian as "having a wonderful, naïve charm that ranks with the best kind of that folk art," with perhaps the best example still standing being the gravestone of John Luther in Warren.[178]

This style of effigy would be repeated over the course of twenty-eight years on gravestones that stand in cemeteries as far from Bristol as Edgartown and Rehoboth, Massachusetts.

Throop's son William Jr. also worked with his father for a time, and their carvings became very popular along the eastern shore of Narragansett Bay. William Throop Jr. also made an effort to carve the more popular motifs of the late eighteenth century, abandoning intricate floral designs for simple urns or a variety of peeking and rising suns like those the Tingley shop was famous for producing.

Contemporaries of these Newport and Bristol carvers would have included Providence stone carvers John Anthony Angel and his brother-in-law, Seth Luther.

Angel was at his most productive in the two decades between 1740 and 1760. While some of his work featured profiles, he eschewed effigies in favor of intricate foliate designs. The gravestones of Hugh Cole (1753) in Warren and Lydia Tew (1751) in Providence are fine examples of his work. Tew's stone, as well as that of Abigail Adams in Providence's Old North Burial Ground, also shows his skill in carving family crests. Angel's lettering was unique in that he mixed upper- and lower-case letters in the script with a flourish that is entirely fluid on the stone.

Seth Luther appears to have become an apprentice to John Angel sometime after his marriage to Angel's sister. While he learned the craft from his father-in-law, he soon expanded the range of his own designs and seems to have had a natural hand for portraiture, becoming well known for his winged effigies, some of which wear remarkable facial expressions.

Within Luther's work, we may find and compare the solemn effigies that adorn the gravestones of Captain Henry Alexander (1758) in South Attleboro, Massachusetts, and Priscilla Cole (1775) in Warren, Rhode Island, with the bemused angel that peers from the gravestone of Captain Benjamin Smith (1759) and the plaited, nearly winking effigy for Esther Whipple (1757), both in Providence.

Several of Luther's carvings may be found in Rumford, Rhode Island's Newman Church Cemetery, but he worked predominately in Providence, his shop being adjacent to the Old North Burial Ground.

John Hartshorn was the earliest carver in Essex County, Massachusetts, but in 1722, at the age of seventy, he moved from Rowley, Massachusetts, to Franklin, Connecticut, to live with his daughter Mary. He soon established a

Tombstone of Captain Christopher Smith, carved by Seth Luther. North Burial Ground, Providence, Rhode Island. *Photo by author.*

shop there and contributed many of the gravestones found in the cemeteries of Franklin, Groton, New London and Norwich, among other towns.

His small but intricately designed stones are easily recognizable. Standing no more than two feet high, they are usually cut in a head-and-shoulders pattern or have three lobed tops, usually decorated with lunettes. His effigies are simple and blank-faced, but his intricate scrollwork and borders of reversed spirals, hearts, loops and geometric designs were an influence on many of the later carvers of eastern Connecticut.

As with many stonecutters', the shop became a family business. The most notable of the Hartshorn carvers would be Stephen Hartshorn, born in 1737, the year of his great-grandfather John's passing, and to him the torch would be passed. He apprenticed from the time he came of age and removed to Providence in 1764 at the age of twenty-eight. His shop offered a variety of designs, carving a number of different winged effigies that ranged from contemplative cherubs to trumpet-blowing angels.

One of Hartshorn's most striking stones is that for William Field (1772), whose double-sided memorial features a winged hourglass on the front of the headstone above the epitaph and, on the back, a peeking sun above his name and the year of his death.

Hartshorn's long-haired angel on the gravestone of Lydia Hartshorn displays exquisite craftsmanship. Examples of his fine relief work may be found on the gravestones of John (1751) and Alice Harding (1762) in Providence, Rhode Island, as well as those of Bathsheba Drew (1767) in Plymouth and Molley Danforth (1769) in Taunton, Massachusetts. The well-known gravestone of Sarah Swan (1767) in Bristol, Rhode Island, features Adam and Eve standing on either side of an apple tree, around which is curled a long serpent, reaching for a fruit in its branches. Hartshorn also has the distinction of having carved seven of the gravestones in the Roger Williams family plot in Providence, now part of Roger Williams Park, created on land donated by Williams's descendants.

Steven Hartshorn's son Charles also entered the trade but was a good deal less prolific and less skilled than his father. Few of his gravestones remain.

A later carver named Franklin Cooley had a shop on Canal Street in Providence and advertised as a dealer in "marble and soapstone." The 1836 city directory also lists a shop on Friendship Street. Cooley's shops produced simplified motifs of the willow and urn design. Others were plain, with simple lettering.

By the closing decades of the nineteenth century, ornamental carvings by draughtsmen on slate were going out of fashion. Marble and limestone effaced slate as the memorial stone of choice, and the gravestone carver's skills were reduced to scroll design and lettering. Granite, which could be smoothed on the face of the gravestone but retain a rugged exterior, also became a popular memorial stone. Slate, on which many of these artists had carved the most delicate portraits and designs, would now only be used for the poor and, at best, receive a name and date of birth and death inscribed, no doubt by an apprentice.

CHAPTER 7

THOSE LOST TO MEMORY

Death on the Poor Farm, Urban Indigents and Common Burial Grounds

Settlements of towns in early New England generally followed the British law that required townspeople to bear the burden of the poor in their community.

Historically, the poor of any community relied on family or neighbors for assistance. Plymouth County instructed towns to keep a herd of cattle that could be farmed out to those in need so they would be provided with milk and other dairy products as well as birthing calves, which would add to the herd while the cows were in their custody.[179]

Other towns bid out the oversight of elderly and infirm inhabitants, a system that left many of the most vulnerable at risk, as we saw in with the unfortunate case of Goodwife Goodwin.

Boston established a poorhouse as early as 1660 but by the eighteenth century had adopted the system of vendue, auctioning off its poor to the lowest bidder.

The town of Malden, Massachusetts, auctioned off Mary Degresha in 1786 for the price of six dollars per week in exchange for providing housing and "proper care."[180] Many of these poor who were "auctioned out" lived little better than the enslaved and indentured laborers who had provided such services for generations.

Many towns adapted the practice of warning out, evicting those who had not proven means of support. While many came to join families in communities, they were still given a timeline within which to find work in a trade or as a laborer for an employer in town. Often families vouched for members, and some were given reprieve, but those who were without family or someone to vouch for them were given notice to leave town.

As the law required, those warned out were removed to the town of their last legal residence, which, by the law, was responsible for their welfare. This sometimes resulted in disputes between towns and, in one case, an episode where a sickly woman was carted from one Rhode Island town to another, being refused at every refuge sought.

These warning outs increased in the years leading up to the Revolutionary War. In South Kingstown, Rhode Island, between 1772 and 1776, the town council spent much of its time allotting the care of infirm persons to relations or neighbors but also brought before the council an increasing number of transients. Most were "removed" to the town of their birth.

In 1772, for example, the town voted that

> *whereas Joseph Larkin…from the Town of Charleston is Poor & become Chargeable to Town…as it doth not appear that he has gaind any legal residence…this Town Council of South Kingstown do adjudge that he the sd Joseph doth belong to ye Town of Charlestown.*[181]

The "Town Serjeant" was ordered to deliver Larkin to his rightful residence. A woman named Joanna Brown was "removed to Providence" that same year.[182]

From then on, the town council saw an increasing number of indigent persons brought before it, some twenty-nine cases in the next three years, involving both individuals and entire families. Despite these efforts to rid the town of "chargeable" persons, the council, and therefore the town, continued to support those who were established inhabitants, such as Content Lee, "an antient woman belonging to this town," or the widow Marberry Potter, whose brother was paid for her care.[183]

Changes in the early nineteenth century created more standards for overseers of the poor, assisting able-bodied people in finding work and housing for those too old or impaired to earn a living. Eventually, when these offices became overwhelmed, almshouses, or poorhouses, began to be built in urban areas.

Urban areas first utilized almshouses to provide shelter for the indigent and elderly, even as all but the infirm continued working in the community. For many years, this system was sufficient, adjusting to the waxing and waning of economic ease and hardship over the years of serving the surrounding community. Once New England's urban populations began to grow, such houses were no longer efficient, and cities sought to build their own tenement-style almshouses to ease overpopulation.

Among the first to be built specifically as an almshouse was Connecticut's Middletown Almshouse, constructed in 1812 on Warwick Street and in use until 1853.[184] The large brick house still stands today as an early example of a gentler form of institutionalization.

The "new" almshouse, constructed in 1854 on the more remote Silver Street, is equally impressive. A 1920s report by the Connecticut State Board of Charities describes the building: "The almshouse is a brick structure, part of which is very old, but it has been kept in good repair and presented an admirable appearance of neatness and good order."[185]

Resting on thirty-five acres of land along the Connecticut River, the property also included the building that housed the old Connecticut Hospital for the Insane.

The town of Norwich built its first almshouse on lower Washington Street, but as the town prospered, wealthy sea captains, merchants and bankers began to build mansions along the now-fashionable boulevard, and the poor of the town were moved into a brick factorylike building constructed on what would be called Asylum Lane.

In the early morning hours of March 12, 1876, a fire broke out in the massive building. As the asylum had purposely been constructed in a remote part of the town, the blaze was beyond control when help finally arrived. Sixteen patients who had been locked in their rooms were unable to escape and perished in the conflagration.[186]

After the fire, the shell of the building was restored and the roof and interior rebuilt. The structure was used for many years, and it is estimated that some 212 individuals who lived and died at the asylum were buried in unmarked graves in a nearby field. Today, a stone marker commemorates their lives:

> *Respectfully dedicated to the 212 Men, Women, and Children*
> *Who Lived and Died at the Norwich Alms House and were Laid*
> *To Rest here between*
> *April 21, 1888*
> *&*
> *July 12, 1927*

Poor farms, or town farms, became a common remedy in rural areas, especially as farmhouses were abandoned by families whose households had gone the way of the mill, seeking employment at one of the many wool and cotton factories that had begun to sprout along the rivers of New England. Almost every rural and suburban community has a Poor Farm Road or Town Farm Road where such places existed.

Often, those farmhouses that were utilized as smallpox hospitals in the mid- to late eighteenth century were later sanitized and used as poor farm houses. If this was not the case, those later poor farms were placed in a nearby location, as the houses used for both purposes were often in isolated parts of the village or town.

In the town of Bedford, Massachusetts, farmer Oliver Pollard conveyed his farmhouse and 118 acres to the town in 1813 for the benefit of the indigent. Over time, citizens of the town who were very old or disabled in some way came to live in the town farm. At times, the rooms were crowded; at other times, as in 1855, when a family of four lived in the house, it was less occupied.

During the 1850s, the farm was overseen by a matron and a superintendent, Abigail and David Constantine. They were successful in making the farm a productive resource for the community. The town farm was an actual working farm, producing primarily milk and potatoes for its own benefit as well as to sell to neighbors. The farm sold timber as well to earn income that would offset the budget afforded each year by the Town Council of Bedford.[187]

Once individuals and families were consigned to an almshouse, town farm or asylum, their lives became anonymous. Little is recorded about the residents of such farms unless they were ill or died. Even in death, the anonymity was carried out, as most were given a simple stone with perhaps a number with which the person could be identified or, most commonly early on, a simple stone with no carving at all.

Today, as one can imagine, the majority of these cemeteries are lost or overgrown. One may find them with some difficulty, a row of carefully placed stones uncovered from leaves and tree litter the most telling sign. Such is the case of the poor farm cemetery in Coventry, Rhode Island, established on a hillside overlooking Hall Pond after 1751. The remaining stones that are still visible are clustered in groups of three or four in a row. The small but documented poor farm cemetery was only recently rediscovered when additions were being planned for an existing housing development. The Joseph Briggs house (1751), which served as the town's poor farm, still stands a short distance from the site. Other sites of historic interest, such as a smallpox hospital used during the Revolutionary War as well as the

Coventry Poor Farm, Briggs farmhouse, 1790. *Photo by author.*

Poor farm cemetery, Portsmouth, Rhode Island. *Courtesy of the Portsmouth Historical Society.*

large farm of Job Greene, where Continental troops encamped between assignments, have long since been lost to newer housing.

Such anonymity for these individuals became greater still with the development of institutions from the mid-nineteenth century into the twentieth, when great Gothic spires and college-like grounds were believed to be the greater solution to a growing population of poor and mentally ill within many counties across the region.

Some such institutions were run successfully, with healthy inhabitants contributing a wide range of craftsmanship and providing produce and surplus products to the community; once those craftsmen and providers died, a numbered stone would be added to the growing row of identical numbered stones.

Over time, however, such places became overcrowded. Disease, especially tuberculosis, ravaged populations, and the numbers of mentally ill individuals admitted to institutions along with others who suffered from still-undiagnosed disabilities increased the risk of abuse and even sexual assaults for vulnerable individuals.

Without family or mourners to claim them, their remains were unceremoniously buried in the "potter's field," as they came to be called.

Other cemeteries, however, are still maintained and even acknowledged by their communities, as is the case with the Almshouse Cemetery in Uxbridge, Massachusetts.

In 1982, when surveyors from the Massachusetts Department of Public Works were mapping out the planned construction route of Interstate 146, they came across a small cemetery on a wooded hillside. The workers, according to archaeologist Ricardo J. Elia, counted sixteen fieldstones, and among them was a marble headstone that "lay face-up and cracked under around an inch of soil."[188] This was the headstone for a remarkable woman of color named Nancy Adams.

In all, thirty-two bodies were recovered from the site, examined at Boston University and all but one relocated to their present hillside grove off a cul-de-sac known as Almshouse Road. The remaining body was determined to be that of an Indigenous man, whose remains were returned to the Nipmuc people.

Such was not the concern in Cranston, Rhode Island, when the state constructed Route 37, a project that was completed in 1968. While state contractors were aware that a portion of an old state institution cemetery lay on the site, they designed an elevated stretch of the highway fifteen to twenty feet above the grave sites. The problem was that the cemetery was far more

Left: Sign for almshouse cemetery, Uxbridge, Massachusetts. *Photo by author.*

Below: Almshouse cemetery, Uxbridge, Massachusetts. *Photo by author.*

extensive than realized and a good portion of the site lay beneath the newly constructed highway.

All was seemingly forgotten until renovations nearly forty years later. As a reconstruction project was getting underway on the northern side of the highway, heavy rains unearthed the remains of seventy-one individuals, interred between 1887 and 1917 and exposed and flushed out of their graves in a heavy rain. State archaeologist Michael Hebert recounted the scene to a reporter:

> *The drainage system had failed and there was erosion at the base of the highway. With the rains, human remains rushed out of the gully into the parking lot where the people who worked at Citizens Bank parked. They go to the parking lot and all these skulls were around their cars.*[189]

The state medical examiner was brought in, who initially believed that construction crews had stumbled on the scene of a grisly crime. While there was a lack of any headstones, workers from the Public Archaeology Laboratory removing the remains soon discovered lead identity plates at nearly every site that would ultimately lead to genealogical testing, enabling officials to notify the next of kin. Those descendants were given the choice of taking the remains for burial elsewhere or allowing the state to reinter their relation.

According to Charles St. Martin of Rhode Island Department of Transportation, the findings were "evidence to the sparse lives these people lived and how they were laid to rest. Along with the skeletal remains, only glass buttons from hospital gowns they were buried in, along with an occasional ring or hair comb, were the only items recovered."[190]

The remains were reinterred in nearby State Institution Cemetery no. 2, but that was not the end of the story. State officials knew that part of the highway had been constructed over the remaining cemetery but kept it quiet. When Maria da Graca—a great-great-granddaughter of Antonio Coehlo, one of the "inmates" of the institution, who had died in 1941—contacted Pegee Malcom, chairwoman of the Rhode Island Historical Cemetery Commission, and then a local television news station, the story came to light. In Malcom's estimation, some eight hundred to one thousand graves were covered with cement and asphalt.

Thankfully, Antonio Coelho's was not among them. His grave had been removed with some 570 other bodies in 1975 to make way for an industrial park just off the highway. The lot where Coelho and others were reburied was overgrown and forgotten, a state marker having been stolen and never replaced. The state eventually replaced the stolen marker with a new, tombstone-like memorial listing all the names of those who had been interred on the site.

In the last chapter of my book *New England Plantations: Commerce & Slavery*, I write of those most marginalized in life—those enslaved workers who contributed to the wealth of the Rhode Island planter economy. In death, they were just as marginalized, as the chapter illustrates with the many forgotten cemeteries where the enslaved were buried. These small cemeteries were usually on the slaveholders' property but separate from the family plot.

When family plots were removed during the advent of the garden cemetery—also a period when many of the old, wealthy families were selling off property—those in the family plot were removed, and the enslaved cemeteries remained to be overgrown and forgotten or, as the chronicler of such plots put it, "lost to the plow."

I begin that last chapter with a story recorded in the diary of "Nailer Tom" Hazard (1756–1845), who wrote of George Coggeshall, a Black man who died suddenly on board a packet ship bound for Providence. As the sun was "in eclipse," the ship anchored off Warwick Neck, and the crew rowed the body to a nearby beach and buried it there.

Months after the book was published, I was reading through a reprint of the nineteenth-century *Narragansett Historical Register*, the original publisher of Hazard's diary in serial form, when I noticed a letter from his descendant Joseph P. Hazard lamenting that his great-uncle, whom he knew as an engaging speaker to young and old, should leave such a "meager, miserable diary."

He also relates the remarkable story "told me more than once" by Hazard of a visit to the house of his friend John Greene, whose property and view from the house overlooked the very beach where he and others had buried Coggeshall's body some thirty years before:

> *On one of my frequent journeys from my house here (at Peace Dale) to Providence on horseback, I stopped for the night at the house of my friend (Greene, I think it was) on Warwick Neck. Next morning, while dressing, I looked out of my chamber window and saw the beach covered with people, who were digging in the sand along the beach in all directions. I could not imagine what the matter was, but on going down stairs to breakfast my friend told me that about a week ago a box containing a human skeleton was worked out by the tide, and these people had been digging ever since for*

the money that Captain Kidd…had buried there, as they believed, and for reason that the skeleton they had found was that of the man he had killed and buried there to watch it.[191]

The body, of course, was that of George Coggeshall, though the Hazard descendant does not remark whether anyone in authority was ever informed of its identity at the time.

CHAPTER 8

EPITAPHS

A s we have seen, funerary art played a key role in displaying what was felt to be the charitable soul of the person that lay beneath the stone. As that art is still most prominently visible on those ancient stones, what has increasingly become lost in the present are the epitaphs carefully carved beneath the name and dates of birth and death of the individual, which, at the time of interment, were as important as the art that adorned the gravestone. Today, many of these epitaphs have lines sunk beneath the soil and, most commonly, many have lines slashed rudely and defaced by Weedwackers, the modern tool of choice for many landscapers, even in cemeteries.

Such epitaphs in early days were the poetry and sayings that reminded visiting families and those strolling by of the fleeting days left to each person, and of the need, even in those pious times, to reflect upon the soul.

Such was the influence of churchyard verses on eight-year-old Thomas Paine that the man who would one day write the prose that stirred men to liberty composed his first known verse in the form of an epitaph to his deceased pet:

> *Here lies the body of John Crow,*
> *Who once was high but now is low*
> *Ye brother crows take warning all*
> *For as you rise so you must fall.*[192]

Perhaps the historian who has conducted the most extensive survey of epitaphs in New England is John G.S. Hanson, who has categorized epitaphs in the region's cemeteries into seven distinct styles and, in his formal studies as well as on his blog, uses examples of the genres and how they evolved over time. These genres are classic, scripture, hymns and psalms, the graveyard school, recurring but unattributed and bespoke.

"The Bible," as Hanson notes, "is a common and unsurprising source of epitaph texts."[193]

While verses on early stones were sparse, especially in rural communities, short Bible verses that would have been familiar to both the family of the deceased and the community of worshippers began to be carved onto memorial stones. These usually consisted of lines of verses taken from the book of Proverbs, Psalms or the book of Ecclesiastes.

Hanson uses the elegantly carved gravestone of Sarah Hopkins in Old Hadley Cemetery as one example. As the wife to two ministers and the mother of fourteen children, her fitting epitaph comes from Proverbs 30:31:

Favor is deceitful and Beauty is vain:
But a woman that feareth the Lord
She shall be praised.[194]

Other lines that would have been well known were those sung in hymns and psalms. As Hanson points out, these lines were not only sung in church services but also "read, memorized, and recited as devotional literature in the home."[195]

Most gravestones held only a single verse of a hymn or psalm, but such was the familiarity of these songs and poetry that the single verse would have brought to mind the entirety of the hymn.

The most popular hymnodist that Hanson has found whose lines became part of epitaphs was Isaac Watts (1674–1748), the famed English Congregational minister and composer, who is credited with writing some 750 hymns.[196]

In the early eighteenth century, a shift occurred with the rising popularity of personalizing the epitaph. An early example would be the Sarah Arnold stone, whose epitaph merges her tragic death with religious undertones. Later epitaphs were more plainly inscribed. The most striking of these involved an account of the deceased's death carved into the gravestone for time immemorial.

Above: Tombstone of Sylvanus Hopkins. North Burial Ground, Providence, Rhode Island. *Photo by author.*

Left: Tombstone of Edward Allen. North Burial Ground, Providence, Rhode Island. *Photo by author.*

One example of such a description is the tombstone of young Sylavanus Hopkins in Providence's North Burial Ground, who was "inhumanely murdered by cruel savages on the 23rd of April, 1743" when he was "cast away on Cape Breton Shore."

In the same burial ground, we find the gravestone of Edward Allen, who was killed in early 1781 by a formerly enslaved man named Prince Greene who had enlisted in the Continental army and was stationed at an encampment in Providence.

Providence was under martial law during much of the war. This meant curfews on taverns and wandering city streets. The soldiers who were stationed in the city were there to both guard its river harbor and uphold that martial law, no matter how unpopular or diverse those who enforced the law might be. Some of those soldiers there to police the streets of Providence were former enslaved men who had enlisted in the Continental army to earn their freedom, like the aforementioned Prince Greene, an enslaved man owned by Richard Greene, an extravagant member of the Greene family, still clinging in the age of the Revolution to an emulation of the English gentry. Prince had twice run away, enlisting in the local militia in 1776 and then in the army to earn his freedom.

On the evening of April 10, 1781, Greene and a handful of others sleeping in the barracks in Providence were awakened by Edward Allen, who, in the company of another man named John Pitcher, began to hurl stones and "illiberal language" at the soldiers inside.[197]

When they were ignored, the two kicked open the door of the barracks. A voice from the darkness warned them to get out before they were fired on. They began to run from the scene, but not before Prince Greene and others followed them outside. Greene was the only one to fire his musket. The ball struck Allen in the back of the head, mortally wounding him.

The incident caused an uproar, especially as a Black soldier had fired a fatal shot at a White resident. As the state's supreme court was in session in Providence at the time, Greene was arrested and brought to trial just four days later.

Greene was defended most ably by David Howell, a friend of Colonel Christopher Greene, commander of Greene's regiment, as well as other high-ranking officers of the Continental army. After a speedy trial, Prince Greene was found "not guilty of willful murder but manslaughter," and he was accordingly branded with an *M* on his hand but allowed to return to the Rhode Island Regiment.[198]

Elizabeth Allen, the victim's mother, was so outraged by what she saw as a lack of justice for her son that she commissioned the Hartshorne gravestone carvers of Newport to furnish his stone, which recounts his "misfortune of being shot by a negro soldier," an act "most barbarously done."[199]

Prince Greene would survive the war but face years of poverty and hardship. Having lost a portion of one foot to frostbite in the last expedition of his regiment to Oswego, he earned a small income playing fiddle for entertainment at dances and quilting parties.

Later epitaphs would include simpler tragedies, as did the 1828 tombstone of twenty-five-year-old Sally C. Robbins, "deceased by a fall from a chaise" in August of that year, as we learn from her elegant, urn-adorned tombstone on Plymouth's Burial Hill.

On the crest of a sloping hill in Providence's Swan Point Cemetery rests a sepulcher that both is unique and tells an interesting story. The tomb holds the body of John Rogers Vinton, a brevet major in the Rhode Island Artillery. Vinton, as the tomb reads, "gallantly fell at the siege of Vera Cruz in Mexico, March 22, 1847." His sepulcher is unique in that the cannonball that brought his death rests atop his tomb.

His last written words, as they are described, are inscribed on the stone in the Latin phrase *Dulce et Decorum est pro Patria Mori*, meaning, "It is sweet and proper to die for one's country." Among the other platitudes inscribed on the tomb is the message that Vinton "was a soldier of the cross. He lived

Tomb of Captain John Rogers Vinton. Swan Point Cemetery, Providence, Rhode Island. *Photo by author.*

and died in the community of the Protestant Episcopal Church. The gentle smile of the Christian here remained on his manly face even in Death."[200]

Indeed, Vinton would have become a minister had not circumstances prevented it from happening. Coming from a privileged family with a long military history, he felt compelled to add to that legacy. Vinton entered the United States Military Academy at the age of fourteen and completed his course of study in just two and a half years. After graduation, he was commissioned as a lieutenant in 1817 and served as aide-de-camp to the general-in-chief of the army, Major General Jacob Brown, from 1825 to 1828. Vinton was made captain of the Third Artillery on December 28, 1835, and later served in Mexico, where he was killed "from the windage of a cannon ball." "The Army is my calling," he had declared in his journal, though he would lose his wife to illness while away at war.[201] After his death, a military outpost in his adopted state of Florida was renamed Fort Vinton.

Captain John Rogers Vinton was well versed in languages, theology and ethics. His journals and letters, along with a biography, were published by the Florida Historical Society in 2017.

The captain's artistic talent was borne out in his striking compositions of the Florida wetlands and portraits of Indigenous Floridians that are still highly prized in collections today.

In the center of the restored almshouse cemetery in Uxbridge, Massachusetts, one stone stands above the rest, which are plain, unmarked or bear simply carved names and dates of birth and death. It is the marble gravestone of Mrs. Nancy Adams, which, though she was part of the poor farm community, was erected after her death in 1859 and bears the epitaph to "a respectable colored woman."

This simple epitaph is the only indication of a truly remarkable story. According to a letter she dictated in 1838 for the abolitionist sisters Sarah and Angelina Grimké, Nancy was born enslaved in eastern Maryland, was married at seventeen to an enslaved man of the plantation and gave birth to two sons and one daughter.[202]

The plantation owner, according to Nancy, had promised that he would not split the family by sale, a common practice among slaveowners. When the slaveholder's wife informed Nancy that he was about to break his promise, she fled with her family into the nearby woods, hid in the hollow of a dead tree and subsisted on acorns. They hid long enough for the master to consent to selling the family to a neighbor instead, with the promise that Adams would be able to buy her freedom.

Marble tombstone of Mrs. Nancy Adams, almshouse cemetery, Uxbridge, Massachusetts. *Photo by author.*

The new master broke his promise as well and sold Nancy and her three children to a plantation owner in Port Gibson, Mississippi. Nancy's daughter died on the journey there, and she and her two sons worked the plantation for more than twenty years. She was sold again, and when her new owner brought her on a trip to Norwich, Connecticut, she escaped again, hiding in an icehouse until he left town.

Nancy lived quietly in Norwich for twelve years before learning that her master had learned of her location and planned her recapture. She fled in her early seventies to Uxbridge, where she lived out her last twenty-one years as a free woman.

Sitting at the crossroads of the Boston Post Road and the Great Road from Worcester to Providence, the town of Uxbridge held a vibrant Quaker community. Being among the first organized abolitionists, they, and a network of Quaker villages along the highway, helped many to reach the safety of free communities in the North. After the passage of the Fugitive Slave Act, this same network would help ferry escaped enslaved people from the South into Canada when the government refused to protect them from slave hunters intent on returning them to their owners for the offered bounty.

Nancy Adams, as her letter to the Grimké sisters indicates, supported these efforts as a free woman, donating to the Massachusetts Anti-Slavery Society and once dictating a letter of gratitude to abolitionist William Lloyd Garrison, delivered along with a "liberal supply of excellent cake."[203]

Nancy Adams led a remarkable life. As she told in the letter she dictated, "I have…tried to give some account of myself but I have not told half that I could tell….My eyes have seen what my tongue dares not speak."[204]

Her story, however, was nearly lost to history.

In 2018, a group of citizens who had been researching Adams's life among those of other formerly enslaved people approached Uxbridge councilwoman Susan Franz with the idea of submitting eleven known sites in town, including the almshouse cemetery, for official recognition as part of the Network of Freedom project on historic sites related to the Underground Railroad operated by the National Park Service.

The Network to Freedom was created in 1998 to help establish a grassroots history of the Underground Railroad, which allows local groups to highlight their area's role in the movement. Based on Nancy Adams's mention in two censuses and the letter she dictated, which was located by researchers among abolitionist papers at the Clements Library at the University of Michigan, her grave was approved as a site of the public history project.

Another remarkable epitaph is etched on all four sides of the obelisk monument to Captain Daniel Drayton in the Rural Cemetery of New Bedford, Massachusetts. Drayton was not a native of New Bedford and only spent much time there toward the end of his life, which ended tragically and unexpectedly in the city's Mansion House hotel on July 1, 1857.

Daniel Drayton grew up in Cumberland County, New Jersey, and recalled in his memoir that as the family lived close to Delaware Bay, "the sight of the vessels passing up and down inspired me with a desire to follow the life of a waterman; though it was some years before I was able to gratify this wish."[205]

By the age of twelve, Drayton had lost his mother, and his father had bound him out to a shoemaker. This and later efforts to learn a trade came to little, and through perseverance, he obtained a position in the timber industry, which allowed him to eventually gain command of a sixty-ton sloop used in the trade and subsequent vessels. He was able to move his family to Philadelphia and establish his business there. As with other maritime trade, risk was a factor, and he lost at least one vessel, but as he recalled, "It was in this coasting business that the best years of my life were spent, during which time I visited most of the ports and rivers between Savannah southward, and St. John, in the British province of New Brunswick, eastward."[206]

On one voyage to the city of Charlestown, South Carolina, after leaving Savannah, Drayton fell severely ill aboard ship and, in the throes of illness, had an epiphany that he needed to return to the Christian upbringing his departed mother had instilled in him at an early age. Once well, he sought spiritual guidance and returned to the water a converted man. As he would write in his memoir after his long career,

> *My trading up and down the Bay…brought me a good deal into contact with the slave population. No sooner indeed, does a vessel, known to be from the north, anchor in any of these waters—and the slaves are pretty adroit*

Obelisk erected to the memory of Captain Daniel Drayton. New Bedford, Massachusetts.
Photo by Jim Grasela.

at determining from what state a vessel comes—than she is boarded, if she remains any length of time, and especially overnight, by more or less of them, in the hopes of obtaining a passage to a land of freedom. During my earlier voyages, several years before, I had turned a Deaf ear to these requests.[207]

Now, as a converted Christian, Drayton saw the plight of enslaved people quite differently and determined that smuggling a few to freedom was one way in which he could allay his fear of "dying in his sins," as he called it. Though he had never attended an abolitionist meeting or read their tracts, Drayton now saw that as "God had made of one flesh all the nations of the earth, I had found out, through intercourse with the negroes, that they had the same desires, wishes, and hopes as myself."[208]

Drayton bristled at children being handed over from families bound by slave owners as soon as they were old enough to be sold. He heard stories of cruelty and rape from the mouths of those who had suffered and seen these deeds and determined that he would save as many souls as he could by conveying them to freedom.

In the summer of 1847, an opportunity presented itself in the form of a Black man who boarded his boat after Drayton had delivered a cache of oysters to the capital city of Washington, D.C. The man wanted passage for his wife and five children. While he was a free man, his wife had labored to pay her master for freedom, but when it came time to settle her emancipation, the owner threatened to sell her.

Drayton agreed to go with the man and visit the family. After doing so, he agreed to transport the family and brought the baggage and bedding aboard by daylight and, that night, smuggled aboard the wife, the children and a niece who accompanied them. The captain then took them on an uneventful ten-day voyage to Frenchtown, where the husband had traveled to greet them. This first successful effort in ferrying enslaved people to freedom emboldened Drayton to undertake a larger and more risky venture.

Word of his exploit had reached the ears of others looking for passage. He received another such request in February while at his home in Philadelphia. After traveling to Washington to meet the man who made the request, he agreed to take on the voyage as soon as a suitable craft was available. He made several requests of owners but was turned down because of the risk of the vessels being confiscated and the fines they would face.

Drayton finally noticed an acquaintance in passing, a Captain Sayres, whose boat, the *Pearl*, was anchored and unused in the harbor. Drayton proposed one hundred dollars to charter the vessel and explained his plan to

Sayres: they would carry as many passengers as they could from Washington to Frenchtown, from where the passengers would be transported to freedom in Philadelphia. According to Drayton, Sayres "fully understood the nature of our enterprise." This time, however, things did not go according to plan when they set sail from Philadelphia.

They proceeded down the Delaware, through the canal at the Chesapeake, making their way to the mouth of the Potomac. They stopped at a small port to purchase twenty cords of wood as a cover cargo and proceeded to Washington, arriving on the night of Thursday, April 13, 1848.

That night, according to Drayton, the was city "in a great state of excitement on the subject of emancipation, liberty, and the rights of man" owing to a great debate held in Congress that very day.[209] Word soon spread of their appearance, and through illicit meetings, it was determined that the passengers would be brought aboard on Saturday night and that they would set sail no later than midnight. It soon became apparent that many more desired passage than was previously known, and Drayton set a strict time of taking on no more passengers after eleven o'clock that evening.

As planned, once the wood was unloaded, Drayton steered the boat to a "lonely place" at a high bank of the river called White House Wharf, where the bank gave some cover and there was only a handful of other buildings nearby.[210]

That Saturday night, some seventy-seven enslaved men, women and children—about equal in distribution, according to Drayton's recollection—were taken aboard the *Pearl*.

Their voyage was slow and sluggish at the outset, and on finding that the prevailing winds kept the vessel from entering the mouth of the Potomac, they anchored in Cornfield Harbor, a popular layover place for vessels to wait out a storm or contrary winds. Drayton had tried to convince Sayres to take the craft farther out to sea, but Sayres believed the vessel unseaworthy with so many aboard. Drayton relented, and in the middle of the night, they were boarded by agents sent from Washington to find the *Pearl* and recover her cargo.

Drayton and Sayres were thrown into prison as a mob outside the jail threatened to lynch them. After the ensuing criminal trial, Drayton was sentenced under two convictions to pay fines amounting to more than $10,000.

Drayton spent four years in the Washington jail before he was pardoned by President Millard Fillmore. While in prison, Drayton had written his memoirs. On release, he found new avenues for his work by speaking at

Oldest known tombstone in Rhode Island. Newman Church Cemetery, East Providence, Rhode Island. *Photo by author.*

abolitionist meetings across New England, which led to his coming to New Bedford in 1857. Despite his success as a speaker, being viewed even then as a kind of hero of abolitionism, Drayton despaired about his hand-to-mouth existence and, in the depths of such despair, took his own life that night in the Mansion House hotel.

His newly found friends and fellow abolitionists from the New Bedford Union Club paid for Daniel Drayton's funeral and the casting and placing of the monument above his grave, where the story of his achievement is etched in stone.

NOTES

Preface

1. William Bradford, *Of Plymouth Plantation 1620–1647*, Samuel Eliot Morison, ed. (New York: Knopf, 1970), 85.
2. My thanks to Cocumscussoc historian Marilyn Harris for this inscription.

Chapter 1

3. Bradford, *Plymouth Plantation*, 156–57, 234.
4. Ibid., 210.
5. James Kendall Hosmer, ed., *Winthrop's Journal: History of New England 1630–1649* (New York, Charles Scribner's Sons, 1908), vol. 1, 125.
6. Ibid., vol. 2, 38.
7. Robert A. Geake, *Colonial New England Curiosities: Remarkable Occurrences, Miracles and Madness* (Charleston, SC: The History Press, 2014), 86.
8. Adrian Tinniswood, *The Rainborowes: One Family's Quest to Build a New England* (New York: Basic Books, 2013), 110.
9. Anthony Vaver, *Early American Criminals: An American Newgate Calendar, Chronicling the Lives of the Most Notorious Criminal Offenders from Colonial America and the New Republic* (Westborough: Pickpocket Publishing, 2014), 9.
10. Joshua Hempstead, *The Diary of Joshua Hempstead 1711–1758* (New London: Collections of the New London County Historical Society Vol. 1, 1901), 28.

11. John Russell Bartlett, ed., *Records of the Colony of Rhode Island and Providence Plantations, in New England 1636–1663* (Providence: FB&C, 2018), 114. Bartlett published ten volumes of this collection during his time as secretary of state from 1855 to 1872.

12. Ibid., 113.

13. Ibid., 156.

14. Ibid.

15. Janet Fletcher Fiske, ed. *Rhode Island General Court of Trials 1671–1704* (Boxford, MA: privately printed, 1998), vol. 1, 12.

16. Dan Klau, "The Rule of Law in Colonial Connecticut," *Appealingly Brief!* (blog), December 20, 2012.

17. Ibid.

18. "Connecticut Code of Laws," Teaching American History, http://teachingamericanhistory.org/document/connecticut-code-of-laws.

19. Ibid.

20. David Hackett Fisher, *Growing Old in America* (New York: Oxford University Press, 1978), 34.

21. Hosmer, *Winthrop's Journal*, vol. 2, 344.

22. Another five accused persons perished in prison.

23. Kettle Hole is now a pond near Slocum, North Kingstown, and the ledge above Wickford referred to by Edgar M. Bacon as "Hell Hollow" is now the site of the Hall's Rock community of condominiums.

24. M.E. Reilly-McGreen, *Witches, Wenches, and Wild Women of Rhode Island* (Charleston, SC: The History Press, 2010).

25. Franklin Bowditch Dexter, ed., *The Literary Diary of Ezra Stiles*, vol. 1 (New York: Charles Scribner's Sons, 1901), 385–86.

26. A member of the grouse family of birds in North America, the heath hen became extinct by 1932.

27. There are numerous versions of this story; the first I came across was in *Haunted New England: A Devilish View of the Yankee Past*, written by Mary Bolte (New York: Random House, 1972), a book I still enjoy.

28. Reilly-McGreen, *Witches, Wenches*, 28.

29. Robert A. Gross, *The Transcendentalists and Their World* (New York: Farrar, Straus and Giroux, 2021), 101.

30. Kathy Weiser-Alexander, Legends of America, https://www.legendsofamerica.com.

31. "That Other New England Witch Hunt," *Before Salem: Witchcraft in Seventeenth Century Connecticut* (blog), October 4, 2009, https://nhcem.wordpress.com/2009/10/04/that-other-new-england-witch-hunt/.

32. "Rebecca Greensmith," *History of American Women* (blog), https://www. womenhistoryblog.com/2008/03/rebecca-greensmith.html.

33. Ibid.

34. Ibid.

35. Ibid.

36. Reilly-McGreen, *Witches, Wenches*, 34.

37. Eve Laplante, *Salem Witch Judge: The Life and Repentance of Samuel Sewall* (New York: Harper Collins, 2007), 151.

38. Ibid., 199–200.

39. "Connecticut Code of Laws," Teaching American History, http:// teachingamericanhistory.org/document/connecticut-code-of-laws.

40. Ibid.

41. Ibid.

42. Simon Middleton and Billy G. Smith (ed.), *Class Matters* (Philadelphia: University of Pennsylvania Press, 2008), 189.

43. One such case involved the whipping of a settler who had enticed a married Indigenous woman into adultery. The sentence of a whipping was carried out to the satisfaction of the wronged husband (Hosmer, *Winthrop's Journal*, vol. 1, 67).

44. Ibid., 69.

45. Ibid.

46. Ibid., 273–74.

47. Janet Fletcher Fiske, ed., *Rhode Island Records of the General Court of Trials* (Boxford, MA: privately printed, 1998), 6.

48. Ibid., 7.

49. Ibid., 14.

50. Ibid.

51. Ibid., 38.

52. Ibid.

Chapter 2

53. *Winthrop's Journal*, vol. 1, 320.

54. The full story of the murder is told in the chapter "Murder and the Mowry Tavern" in my earlier book *Historic Taverns of Rhode Island* (Charleston, SC: The History Press, 2011).

55. James Arnold, in his *Narragansett Historical Register Vol. 1*, writes that House's murder was "likely to have taken place somewhere between Richard

Smith's house (Smith's Castle) and the Devil's Foot (the long granite ledge that stretched west of the Post Road and was the seat of the Narragansett Sachem Canonicus)." *Narragansett Historical Register* (Providence, 1882; reprint by Heritage Press, 1994), 164.

56. *Rhode Island Court Records 1662–1670*, vol. 2 (Providence: Rhode Island Historical Society, 1922).

57. Ibid., 98.

58. Elaine Forman Crane, *Killed Strangely: The Death of Rebecca Cornell* (Ithaca, NY: Cornell University Press, 2002), 17.

59. Ibid.

60. Ibid.

61. Ibid., 109.

62. Fiske, *General Court of Trials*, 32.

63. Ibid.

64. As reprinted in "Connecticut Justice: When Murder Became Manslaughter in 1712," New England Historical Society, https://newenglandhistoricalsociety.org.

65. Wilkins Updike, *Memoirs of the Rhode Island Bar* (Boston, 1842), 58–62

66. Ibid.

67. Ibid.

68. Ibid

69. Ibid.

70. Rev. Jacob Bailey, *The Frontier Missionary: A Memoir of the Life of Rev. Jacob Bailey, A.M.* (New York: Stanford & Swords 1853), 16–22

71. Kenneth Carlson, "List of Executions in Rhode Island, 1670–1845," *The Online Review of Rhode Island History* (blog), smallstatebighistory.com, June 12, 2021.

72. Ibid.

73. Kenneth Carlson, *List of Executions…*, *General Treasurer Accounts*, August 1751.

74. Tinniswood, *Rainborowes*, 189–90.

75. Hosmer, *Winthrop's Journal*, vol. 2, 317–18.

76. Ibid.

77. Ibid.

78. Vaver, *Early American Criminals*, 38–41.

79. Ibid., 39

80. Ibid.

81. Ibid., 41.

82. Ibid., 119–20.

83. Hempstead, *Diary*, 616–19.

84. Carolyn Marvin, *The Hanging of Ruth Blay: An Eighteenth-Century New Hampshire Tragedy* (Charleston, SC: The History Press, 2010), 44.

85. Ibid., 52–55.

86. Ibid., 60.

87. Ibid.

88. Ibid., 76.

89. Ibid.

90. Ibid.

91. "Six Places Where a Gallows Once Stood," New England Historical Society, accessed October 16, 2022, http://newenglandhistoricalsociety.com.

92. Alberton, *Class Matters*, 191.

93. Carlson, "List of Executions."

94. "The Murder of Amasa Sprague, and the Irishman Persecuted for the Crime," New England Historical Society, accessed November 30, 2022, http://newenglandhistoricalsociety.com. For a more comprehensive reading of the murder and trial, see Paul F. Caranci's *The Hanging and Redemption of John Gordon* (Charleston, SC: The History Press, 2012).

Chapter 3

95. Hosmer, *Winthrop's Journal*, vol 2, 18.

96. Ibid., 32.

97. Ibid., 30.

98. Ibid., 28–29.

99. Robert A. Geake, *Colonial New England Curiosities* (Charleston, SC: The History Press, 2014), 110.

100. *Rhode Island Court Records*, 29.

101. Robert A. Geake, "So Neare as We Can Judge: Jury Duty in Early Rhode Island," *The Online Review of Rhode Island History* (blog), February 4, 2016, http://smallstatebighistory.com/so-neare-as-we-may-judge-jury-duty-in-early-rhode-island/.

102. *Rhode Island Roots Genealogical Catalogue*, 195–96.

103. Geake, "So Neare."

104. Ibid.

105. "The History of Epidemics in New England," New England Historical Society, accessed October 11, 2022, http://newenglandhistoricalsociety.com.

106. Ibid.

107. Dexter, *Diary of Ezra Stiles*, 218–19.

108. Ruth Wilder Sherman, FASG ed., *Peleg Burroughs Journal 1778–1798: The Tiverton R.I. Years of the Humbly Bold Baptist Minister* (Rhode Island Genealogical Society, 1981), 32–34.

109. Hempstead, *Diary*, 42.

110. C.D. Barrows, ed., *The Diary of John Comer*, Collections of the Rhode Island Historical Society, Vol. 3 (Providence, 1893), 54.

111. A rail-enclosed platform without such a cupola was called a "captain's watch," a place for a retired mariner to look for the safe return of vessels he had invested in or owned outright.

112. Hosmer, *Winthrop's Journal*, vol. 2, 60–61.

113. Vaver, *Early American Criminals*, 50–51.

114. Ibid.

115. Barrows, *Diary of John Comer*, 42.

116. Ibid.

117. Robert E. Shalhope, *A Tale of New England: The Diaries of Hiram Harwood, Vermont Farmer, 1810–1837* (Baltimore, MD: Johns Hopkins University Press, 2003), 136–37.

118. "History of Connecticut Newspapers," Connecticut state library website, http://ctstatelibrary.org.

119. See Robert Geake, "Unfortunate Ends: Gleanings from the Death Notices in Early Rhode Island Newspapers," *The Online Review of Rhode Island History* (blog), http://smallstatebighistory.com.

Chapter 4

120. Hosmer, *Winthrop's Journal*, vol. 1, 294.

121. Adolph B. Benson, ed., *Peter Kalm's Travels in North America* (New York: Dover, 1964), 669.

122. Aislinn Sarnacki, "The 1st Documented Haunting in the U.S. Happened in 18th Century Hancock County," *Bangor Daily News*, August 14, 2021 (original story appeared in 2015).

123. Thomas D'Agostino and Arlene Nicholson, *Strange New England* (Charleston, SC: The History Press, 2021), 143.

124. Ibid.

125. Reverend Abraham Cummings, *Immortality Proved by the Testimony of Sense: In Which Is Contemplated the Doctrine of Spectres and of the Existence of a Particular Spectre Addressed to the Candor of an Enlightened Age* (Portland: J.R. Lovell, 1859), 31.

126. Ibid., 32.

127. Ibid.

Chapter 5

128. Alice Morse Earle, *Customs and Fashions of Early New England* (New York: Charles Scribner's Sons, 1983), 662.

129. Joshua Hempstead, *Diary of Joshua Hempstead of New London, Connecticut Covering a Period of Forty-Seven Years from September, 1711 to November, 1758* (New London, The New London County Historical Society, 1901), 7–9.

130. Thomas Lechford, *Plain Dealing, or Newes from New England* (Boston: J.K. Wiggin & W.P. Lunt, 1867; reprinted from original edition of 1639).

131. Ibid.

132. Burroughs, like many itinerant clergy at the time, was employed by several towns and thus divided his ministerial work among widely spread parishoners.

133. Robert Geake, ed., *Fired a Gun at the Rise of the Sun: The Diaries of Private Noah Robinson of Attleboro Massachusetts* (privately printed, 2018).

134. Earle, *Customs and Fashions*, 665.

135. Bury wills and inventories, Camden Society Collections. See also William Jones, *Finger-Ring Lore* (London, 1890), 355–89.

136. Translates literally as "rises or dies."

137. Translates as "love unites all."

138. Earle, *Customs and Fashions*, 667.

139. Ibid., 670.

140. Ibid.

141. Sarah Hoile, "Objects of Love and Loss: Mourning Jewelry," Museum of London, https://www.museumoflondon.org.uk/discover/objects-love-and-loss-mourning-jewellery.

142. Lillian B. Miller, *The Puritan Portrait: Its Function in Old and New England*, Colonial Society of Massachusetts.

143. David Jaffe, *A New Nation of Goods: The Material Culture of Early America* (Philadelphia: University of Pennsylvania Press, 2010), 226.

144. See Robert A. Geake, "Casting Some Light on the Early Lumineers," *Cocumscussoc Review*, December 2022, https://smithscastle.org.

145. Jaffe, *New Nation of Goods*, 226.

146. Ibid., 230.

147. Margaret M. Coffin, *Death in Early America* (New York: Thomas Nelson, 1976), 100.

148. When many family burial grounds were disinterred for removal to a new community "garden cemetery," these metal plates were often the only trace found from a burial that had taken place a century or more ago.
149. Coffin, *Death*, 105.
150. Ibid., 101.
151. Ibid., 114.
152. Ibid., 117.
153. Dexter, *Diary of Ezra Stiles*, vol. 1, 236.
154. Coffin, *Death*, 127.
155. See Phipps/Historic Burying Grounds/City of Boston at http:// cityofboston.gov.
156. Mary Maynard, *Dead and Buried in New England* (Concord, NH: Yankee Books, 1993), 13.
157. Ibid.
158. Coffin, *Death*, 129.
159. Ibid.
160. Susan E. Maycock and Charles M. Sullivan, *Building Old Cambridge, Architecture and Development* (Cambridge: MIT Press, 2016), 434–39.
161. Ibid.
162. Trudy Irene Scee, *Garden Cemeteries of New England* (Bangor: Down East Books, 2016), 38–39.
163. George J. Harris, *A Visitation to the Cemeteries of Ancient Kingstowne*, vol. 1. Handwritten book in the collection of the Rhode Island Historical Society's Robinson Library.
164. Robert A. Geake, *The Road Less Traveled: Forgotten Historic Highways of New England* (Charleston, SC: Arcadia Publishing, 2019), 90–94.
165. Ibid.

Chapter 6

166. Coffin, *Death*, 147.
167. Ibid., 150.
168. John E. Sterling, "How Much Did They Cost? Answers and Musings on Early Newport Gravestones," *Rhode Island Roots* 36, no. 4: 181.
169. Ibid.
170. James Blachowicz, "The Carvers of Kingston, Massachusetts," *Markers XVIII* Association for Gravestone Studies (2001): 71.
171. Ibid., 98.

172. Ibid., 81.

173. Ibid., 114–15.

174. Coffin, *Death*, 156–57.

175. Julian Mendoza, "Gravestone Art's Beauty Subject of Historic Deerfield Tours," *Greenfield Reporter*, October 31, 2021.

176. Vincent Luti, "Gravestone Carvers of the Narragansett Basin," *Markers* 22 (1999).

177. H.M. Forbes, *Gravestones of Early New England and the Men Who Made Them* (Princeton, NJ: Pyne Press, 1973), 97.

178. Luti, "Gravestone Carvers," 102.

Chapter 7

179. "A Poorhouse in Each New England State," New England Historical Society, accessed September 28, 2022, http://newenglandhistoricalsociety. org.

180. Ibid.

181. Jean C. Stutz, *South Kingstown Rhode Island Town Council Records 1771–1795* (Kingston, RI: Pettasquamscut Historical Society, 1988), 10.

182. Ibid.

183. Ibid., 42

184. Michael Westerfield, "The History of Connecticut Poorhouses," http://connecticutpoorhouses.info.

185. Ibid.

186. Ibid.

187. Ouligon/Corey, "The Bedford Almshouse or Poor Farm," *Bedford Citizen*, April 8, 2014, http://thebedfordcitizen.org.

188. Ibid.

189. Jay Adams, "Rehabilitation of Rt. 37 Unearths Long-Forgotten Cemetery, http://constructionequipmentguide.com." December 10, 2009, http://constructionequipmentguide.com.

190. Ibid.

191. James N. Arnold, *Narragansett Historical Register*, vol. 1 (Heritage Books, 2015), 296–97.

Chapter 8

192. Craig Nelson, *Thomas Paine: Enlightenment, Revolution, and the Birth of Modern Nations*, 18.

193. John G.S. Hanson, "A Guide to Reading Early Epitaphs," accessed October 17, 2022, https://www.johnhansonauthor.com/a-guide-to-reading-early-epitaphs.

194. Ibid.

195. Ibid.

196. "Isaac Watts, Father of English Hymnody," *Christianity Today*, August 8, 2008, http://christianitytoday.com.

197. Robert A. Geake, *From Slaves to Soldiers* (Yardley, Westholme, 2016), 105–6.

198. Ibid.

199. Ibid. I am also indebted to Prof. Robert Emlin, whose talk "A Grievance Immortalized" at the John Carter Brown Library (April 28, 2016) gave me further information on this episode.

200. See http://www.famousamericans.net/johnrogersvinton/.

201. Ibid.

202. Sabrina Imbler, "The Grave of Nancy Adams, Who Thrice Escaped Slavery, Is Now a Symbol of Freedom," Atlas Obscura, accessed November 3, 2022, http://atalsobscura.com/articles/nancy-adams-underground-railroad-massachusetts.

203. Ibid.

204. Ibid.

205. Daniel Drayton, *Personal Memoir of Daniel Drayton for Four Years and Four Months a Prisoner (For Charity's Sake) in Washington Jail, Including a Narrative of the Voyage and the Capture of the Schooner Pearl* (New York: American and Foreign Anti-Slavery Society, 1855).

206. Ibid.

207. Ibid., 12.

208. Ibid.

209. Ibid., 16.

210. Ibid., 17.

INDEX

ABOUT THE AUTHOR

R obert A. Geake is a public historian and the author of fourteen books on Rhode Island and New England history, including *From Slaves to Soldiers: The First Rhode Island Regiment in the American Revolution*. Other books include *A History of the Narragansett Tribe of Rhode Island: Keepers of the Bay*, *Native and New Americans*, *New England's Citizen Soldiers: Mariners and Minutemen* and *Fired a Gun at the Rising of the Sun: The Journal of Noah Robinson of Attleboro in the Revolutionary War*. He is currently working on another book, to be titled *The Battle Off the Field*. Geake currently serves on the board of trustees of the Cocumscussoc Association, which maintains Smith's Castle historic house museum in North Kingstown, Rhode Island. He also serves on the advisory board of the Rhode Island Slave History Medallion project. Geake is a contributor to the blogs *The Online Review of Rhode Island History* (smallstatebighistory.com), and, most recently, The Cocumscussoc Review on smithscastle.org. His essay on Rhode Island and the American Revolution is among those contributed to EnCompass, online tutorials for the Rhode Island Historical Society and the Rhode Island Department of Education.

Visit us at
www.historypress.com
···